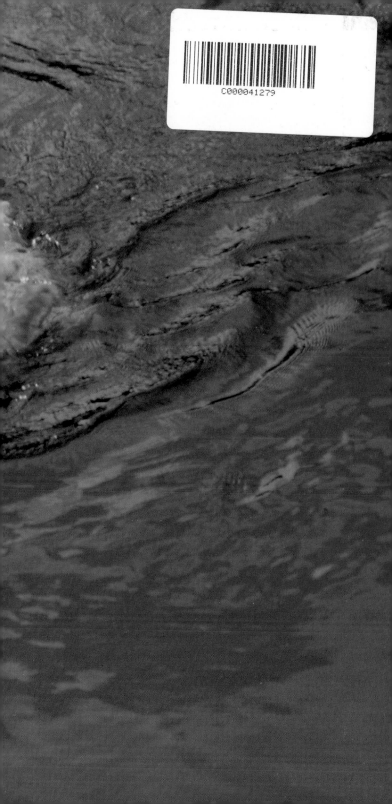

A *PetLove* Guide to

Golden Retrievers

A *PetLove* Guide to

Golden Retrievers

All you need to know about your Golden Retriever,
including health care, training, breeding and showing

Marigold Timson

A *PetLove* Guide

Distributed to the pet trade by Interpet Ltd.,
Vincent Lane, Dorking, Surrey RH4 3YX.

Credits

Editor: Jo Finnis
Designers: Geoff Denney and Philip Gorton
Photographs: Marc Henrie
Contributor: Catherine Zingg
(chapter on Working Golden Retrievers)
Veterinary consultant: Robert A Cathcart, BSc, MRCVS
US consultants: Hal and Mary Sundstrom; Seymour N Weiss
Colour origination: Magnum Graphics Ltd., and Pixel Tech Ltd.
Typesetting: The Old Mill and SX Composing DTP.
Printed in China by Leefung Asco Printers Ltd.

Contents

Author

Marigold Timson bred and showed Golden Retrievers for over 30 years
under the 'Gyrima' affix. Sadly, she died in 1991. She owned and bred nine
English champions and many more around the world. She was international
judge, judging in Australia, Norway, Sweden, Denmark, Finland, Germany
and Switzerland. She was a member of The Kennel Club and served on The
Executive Committee of the Golden Retriever Club for many years. This
revised edition has been kindly updated by Marigold Timson's daughter,
Joanna, who has followed in her late Mother's footsteps.

Foreword

Since I wrote the Foreword for the first edition of this book, we have all been saddened by Marigold's sudden and untimely death in April 1991, ending her 30 year love for and abounding interest in the Golden Retriever.

My husband and I first met Marigold at our first dog show in the early 60s. This first meeting developed into a long friendship, during which time Marigold's willingness to listen, advise and comfort has helped me through the 'ups and downs' of showing and breeding Goldens. I have so much missed being able to pick up the phone, talk to her and to be given her no-nonsense and 'to the point' comments, and I know many of her friends throughout the breed feel the same.

Marigold always took great care in the presentation of her dogs for the show ring but they were also her treasured friends.

Whether you are buying your first Golden, breeding for the first time or are an expert, through this book, Marigold has left us a legacy of her love, knowledge and experience to help Golden owners care for and understand this delightful breed.

Brenda Lowe

Photographer

Marc Henrie began his career as a Stills man at the famous Ealing Film Studios in London. He then moved to Hollywood where he worked at MGM, RKO, Paramount and Warner Brothers, photographing the Hollywood greats: Humphrey Bogart, Edward G Robinson, Gary Cooper, Joan Crawford and Ingrid Bergman, to name a few. He was one of the last photographers to photograph Marilyn Monroe.

Later, after he had returned to England, Marc specialized in photographing dogs and cats, rapidly establishing an international reputation. He has won numerous photographic awards, including the Kodak Award for the Best Animal Photograph and the Neal Foundation Award for Outstanding Photography of Animal Behaviour.

Authors' acknowledgments

The author would like to thank the following people for their help with photography: Catherine Zingg, Mr Robert A Cathcart, BSc, MRCVS, the Morss family, Mrs and Miss Birkin, Miss Gill and Mrs Philpott, Mr and Mrs David Andrews and L Kipps. Also, grateful thanks to Miss Phyllis Southwell for permission to reproduce photographs from Mrs Elma Stonex's archives and the Kennel Club for permission to reproduce the breed standards.

Introduction

Golden is a family dog; it likes to participate in every aspect of life, be it playing with the baby, football, swimming, surfing. They will always be at the fore, enjoying the family's company. They crave love and affection, and the more they are included in your activities the closer they become to you and are very biddable. Companionship is their top priority; they would rather go without food than love even though they are born gannets! On quiet evenings, they also become part of the hearthrug.

Characteristics

The Golden Retriever is a thoroughly adaptable, multi-purpose dog. Goldens were originally bred to be gundogs. They are also now used as guide dogs, PAT and sniffer dogs, as well as helping with the disabled. You can enjoy the many facets of your Golden by combining the role of family pet with showing, gundog, obedience and agility work. Handsome, good tempered, intelligent and aware of your every need, they give more pleasure than you can possibly return.

Now for the distinct drawbacks of owning a Golden, but the humorous side as well. You must accustom yourself to receiving many unusual presents — a display of those natural retrieving instincts — such as cushions, tea-towels, oven gloves and other household objects. I have even shudderingly received carving knives! Accept these politely and civilly and give your dog a present such as a

Above: *Goldens and children form close friendships, teaching the young responsibility for other beings. Eager to join games, Goldens become an integral part of family life.*

biscuit or his toy. Always remember that this behaviour is natural and instinctive, so it is unfair to chastise. The family will become incredibly tidy or they will have no socks or shoes to wear, and even the dirty laundry will be retrieved from the bathroom!

Goldens love a spot of gardening. While you plant they will follow digging up. They love cooking, sitting beneath the work surface collecting the scraps. It is advisable to keep any kitchen work surfaces clear and food high up out of reach, or you may lose your meal! Goldens are sometimes thieves, but they are also amazingly obstinate and deaf. They love swimming and, if deprived, the craving can extend to the dirtiest, saucer-sized puddle!

Another typical characteristic that you must understand is their habit of 'talking', not to be confused with growling. They can carry on a conversation with you, from guttural to soprano tones, so loudly that you can hardly hear yourself speak. One well-known kennel once had three champion bitches who would put on a great performance, on request: a choir with three different tones, directed by their choirmaster-owner with much amusement. You really can have so much fun with your Goldens.

Responsibilities
Never forget your Golden is a dog and not a human-being, as he would have you believe. A dog does not need to sleep on your bed nor on your sofa. He does not need titbits from the table, and if there are leftovers they should be fed as part of the dog's dinner, not as an extra. Goldens become overweight very easily. The dog should be expected to be well-mannered in your home and not monopolize the company, just as you would not tolerate a badly behaved child in the same situation.

Ownership of a Golden, or indeed any other dog, also includes responsibility to the general public. You must contain him in a well-fenced garden or yard. If your garden is too large to fence, then the dog must have a small area fenced for himself. He must be trained to behave in public, not to jump at people and to walk in an orderly fashion on the lead. You must be responsible for clearing up his excrement whilst exercising. Always have a plastic bag in your pocket for this purpose and dispose in the nearest litter bin. When away from your home, your dog should always wear a collar with a name and address tag — your surname not the dog's, otherwise it could be enticed away by someone calling his name. Pets are stolen only too often.

Help on selection
If by now you have decided a Golden is for you, then visit a show where you can see a large number of them (your national kennel club will be able to give you details — see the Appendix). This will narrow your choice to the type and colour you prefer, and there is considerable variety. Talk to the breeders; you will find them a friendly and helpful group of people absolutely dedicated to and besotted with the breed. They will answer all your questions to enable you to understand the breed.

Now that I have prepared you for the joys of owning and being owned by a Golden, I shall proceed to the choice and care of your puppy, both now and in later years.

Chapter One

ORIGINS OF THE GOLDEN RETRIEVER

Until 1959, the popular belief was that the Golden Retriever originated from a troupe of Russian circus dogs supposed to have been purchased by Lord Tweedmouth during a visit to Brighton (England) and taken back to Guisachan, his estate in Scotland. Certainly, dogs similar to the old yellow retrievers have been seen in Russia for over a century and were used both as sheepdogs and gundogs. Many people also believed that yellow retrievers had been bred from other coloured retrievers; sandy, yellow, liver and brown were known and yellows could be produced from black parents.

Lord Tweedmouth
It is certain that Guisachan was the birthplace of the Golden Retriever and how fortunate that the first Lord Tweedmouth kept methodical stud books and records which establish the true facts and origins of the breed. Mrs Elma Stonex spent ten years in researching these facts and in 1959, the sixth Lord Ilchester (Lord Tweedmouth's great nephew) and Mrs Stonex presented

Below: *Guisachan, Lord Tweedmouth's Scottish Estate, the birthplace of Golden Retrievers, today in decay.*

the true facts to the Kennel Club in England, which were officially recognized and are now recorded at the Kennel Club's offices in Clarges Street, London.

In fact, the first Lord Tweedmouth did indeed purchase a yellow wavy-coated retriever called Nous from a cobbler in Brighton, who in turn had been given it by a gamekeeper of Lord Chichester. He did indeed take it back to Guisachan where he bred it with a Tweed Water Spaniel (Belle) from Ladykirk on the Tweed. From this mating stem all Golden Retrievers.

There does not appear to be much information about the Tweed Water Spaniel. These dogs seem to have originated around the banks of the Tweed, varying in colour from liver to yellow, with tight, curly coats. They may have been descended from the Water-dog of tawny colour inhabiting the Northumbrian coast and also the east coast around Grimsby and Yarmouth. These were ships' dogs and would swim out to sea carrying a line and tow the ship in, sometimes saving ships' crews from wrecks. Reports from the past say that the Tweed Water Spaniel strongly resembled the Water-dogs; it was more like a Retriever than a Spaniel in appearance. It was reported that the Water-dogs had been crossed with the Newfoundland for additional strength.

Lord Tweedmouth's records cover the period from 1868 until 1889, and he constantly line-bred to the original mating of Nous and Belle in 1868, although occasionally he resorted to an outcross. From this first mating he retained two bitches, Cowslip and Primrose. A third bitch, Ada, was given to the fifth Earl of Ilchester and founded the Ilchester strain in which black outcrosses were often used. The only dog, Crocus, was given to the second Lord Tweedmouth, then the Hon. Edward Marjoribanks. Cowslip was mated to Tweed (also a Tweed Water Spaniel), who also came from Ladykirk, and Topsy was retained from the litter. Topsy was mated to Sambo — presumed to be a black Flat or Wavy-coated Retriever — and Zoe was kept from the litter.

Cowslip was then mated again, this time to Sampson, a Red Setter belonging to Lord Tweedmouth's son, and produced Jack and Gill (1875). In 1884, the two Nous lines through Cowslip were joined by mating Jack, Cowslip's son, to Zoe, Cowslip's granddaughter. Zoe whelped four yellow puppies and a dog, Nous II, and two bitches, Gill II and Tansway, were kept — Cowslip and Nous I appearing three times in four generations. Zoe also had another two litters to Sweep (referred to as 'Bred by Lord

Below: *Mrs Stonex discovered this drawing of a Northumbrian Water-dog, which the Tweed Spaniel strongly resembled.*

Ilchester – Crocus Breed'), all of which were yellow puppies.

By this time, Lord Tweedmouth decided to outcross and mated Gill II to Tracer, a black Flat or Wavy-coated Retriever, full brother to Ch Moonstone, also black, but a line noted for producing red puppies. This was catastrophic – ten black puppies! One of these black puppies (Queenie) was mated back to Nous II (yellow), line-breeding, as Queenie's dam (Gill) and Nous II were litter brother and sister, giving four lines back to the Nous/Belle mating. Success! This produced two yellow Retrievers, Prim and Rose, whelped 1889. These were the last records kept by Lord Tweedmouth who died in 1894. Although the record was lost, Lord Ilchester remembered Lord Tweedmouth using a sandy Bloodhound cross in the 1890's. The progeny were darker coloured, very big, powerful, ugly, definitely hound-like and of dubious temperament.

Early pedigrees

Puppies born at Guisachan that were not retained were given to keepers on neighbouring estates, relatives and friends. One of the family keepers sold two puppies to Viscount Harcourt (Culham Kennel) whose dam was Lady belonging to Archie Marjoribanks (Tweedmouth's youngest son). She could have been a daughter of Prim or Rose but she was born at Guisachan around 1891 and from her descended Culham Brass, who is behind all early pedigrees.

Several other Guisachan-bred Goldens are behind early pedigrees, such as Conon, sire of Proud Ben (1900), who through his grandchildren is a forebear of Heydown Kennel. Conon also sired several Culhams.

Rock was another important Tweedmouth sire behind Wavetree Sam, his son, originally unregistered Faithful Sam, and both his names are behind early pedigrees. Sam was the sire of Ingestre Tyne (Mr MacDonald) and when mated to Ingestre Scamp,

Above: *A delightful painting of the puppy, Saucy of Buckhold, Normandy Black-eyed Susan and Silence of Tone.*

Right: *Last yellow Retrievers recorded by Lord Tweedmouth, extended from the KC Stud Book with colours and breeds used.*

produced Yellow Nell, dam of Mrs Charlesworth's early dog, Normanby Sandy.

All present day Goldens stem from Guisachan breeding and we are greatly indebted to the late Elma Stonex for her keen researching into origins and pedigrees.

There are few people today who grasp the principle of line-breeding and Lord Tweedmouth must be admired for his instinctive and intuitive knowledge of genes and his positive approach to breeding our much loved Golden Retriever.

Chapter Two

THE GOLDEN RETRIEVER PUPPY

How and where to buy

The secretaries of Golden Retriever Breed Clubs (see Appendix) will keep a list of members' puppies for sale. This is a good source of information, since they will have made sure that the parents' hips have been X-rayed and scored, and that they hold up to date eye certificates (see Chapter Five).

Word of mouth has a lot to do with selling. Someone buys a puppy from an experienced breeder, someone else admires it and asks where it was purchased and so the chain goes on. Reputable breeders have many puppy enquiries, usually have stud dogs and know where puppies have been born.

Be careful of local advertisements. See the mother with her pups and ask to see relevant certificates for hips and eyes. Beware the mixed breeding kennels where puppies

Below: *Happy seven-week puppies; mother supervises behaviour and toilet training, but no longer provides food.*

were probably not born on the premises but perhaps brought long distances from big puppy farms at a very tender age.

I cannot stress too highly the importance of buying from a reputable breeder and taking advice from a breed club Secretary. It is a sad fact that it costs as much to buy a good-looking, healthy puppy as a poor specimen which may develop health or temperament problems in the first year.

It is advisable to book a puppy provisionally before birth since they are so popular. Visit your prospective breeder and have a look at the dam and sire if possible. Your breeder will want to know a lot about you, your family, fencing, whether you work and how long the puppy would be on its own. Breeders do not sell puppies to anyone on request. They want to ensure that the puppy will have a happy home and will be well cared for.

It takes a lot of work and care to produce a puppy for you to take home at seven to eight weeks.

Breeders give a unique after-sales service, and problems can be solved by a telephone call.

Choosing your puppy

Your first decision must be whether you have a male or female. Unlike some breeds, temperament in Goldens should be the same in the male or female. The males are very handsome and have a lot of character and fun in their makeup. My first Golden was a male and my children had a great deal of fun with him. Although we lived on an open-plan estate, he never strayed from the front lawn. As long as they are content with their family life and are not used at stud, that is how male Goldens should be. If they are used at stud, they will need a steady supply of bitches to keep them happy.

Below: *Illustrating the wide colour range in Goldens (cream to darkest gold) and their keen interest in gardening.*

If you choose a bitch you should be aware of your responsibilities to the neighbourhood, and be prepared to restrict her to home and garden or yard when on heat. The family must understand that the back or the front gate must be kept shut and bolted at all times. Do not take bitches on heat for walks away from your home or you will have a pack of male dogs following the scent back to your home and they will set up camp for the entire season! If you must go for walks, take her in the car away from your home and then walk.

Chlorophyll tablets are quite effective in keeping the local canine rapists off the scent. A bitch is far more likely to go in search of a husband than a dog unused at stud. They have strong maternal instincts and are very hormonal at these times.

You must also decide on your colour preference: cream, pale gold, mid-gold or very dark.

Breeders vary in their attitude to puppy buyers. Some prefer not to have you visit until the puppies are ready to leave, because they fear the risk of infection. I prefer to meet puppy buyers almost immediately the puppies are born, after taking effective precautions in spraying runs and kennels with parvo deterrent mixes. I advise another visit at four weeks, when the puppies are walking, and finally at seven weeks you can come and choose your puppy and take it home. However, when visiting any breeder, you should always wear clean clothes which have not been near other animals, you should not have come straight from a show and you should have disinfected your shoes with a solution of bleach and a non-toxic disinfectant.

This contact gives me the opportunity to assess you, your family and the temperament you require in the puppy. The older person who has recently lost a 14-year old certainly does not need a boisterous puppy. They will have forgotten the hard work of a puppy and the fact that they are themselves 14 years older. Nor does a young boisterous family want a quiet puppy. Their need is for one who has enough resilience to combat family life.

Apart from having a family pet, there are a lot of activities you can enjoy with your Golden, such as showing (see below), gundog working, obedience and agility. If you are interested in any of these, confide in your breeder and she or he will be able to guide you to the right puppy with these potentials in mind. Whilst the final choice is based on a very personal attraction, you would be well-advised to talk it through with your breeder and take her or his advice.

When you come to look at the litter at seven weeks, you should expect to see an even litter in terms of the size of the puppies; they should be fat and happy, wagging their tails and hoping to greet you for a friendly hug and pat. You should also expect to see clean, airy kennels with well-scrubbed, clean runs and exercise areas.

Choosing a show puppy
If you are seriously interested in showing and breeding, I cannot stress too highly that you should approach the successful breeders and state your purpose. I suggest you go to breeders who are not only successful themselves but sell puppies that are successful when shown by other people and novices. While you should take their advice, since they have knowledge of their breeding, you must look for a quality puppy standing out from the others with that additional 'star' quality.

It should have a balanced head for its age, very dark eyes and pigmentation. A guide to pigmentation that will be permanent is to look in the roof of the mouth — it is a better guide than the nose and pads. The breed standard specifies a scissor bite, and you will require a really good scissor bite at this age to allow for jaw growth. A straight front is a good start and if you put your hand between the front legs it should feel a good fit, not with room for two

Above: *An excellent example of dark pigment in the roof of the mouth, a more accurate guide than the nose and pads.*

Below: *The scissor bite called for by the breed standard. Never breed from a bad mouth — it is very hard to eradicate.*

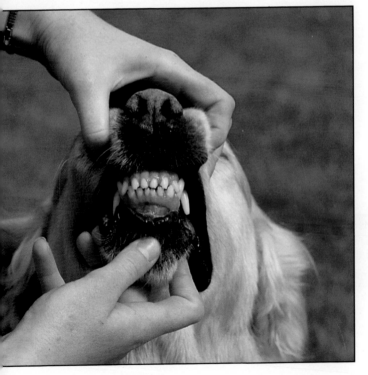

hands! The shoulders should be placed well behind the front legs and as specified in the breed standard. A strong, level topline, good tailset, well-angulated stifles and hocks should complete the picture (see page 68). When on the move, the puppy should have good head carriage from a neck in proportion with his body. He should show potential of fulfilling the breed standard (see Appendix).

Papers

When you collect your puppy you should be presented with a full diet and general information sheet, together with full pedigree and individual registration certificate. That is if the breeder has registered the litter, and most reputable breeders register all their puppies, ensuring they carry their prefix (or family name) of which they are justly proud. Do NOT on any account deviate from your breeder's diet sheet as this would upset your puppy's routine and also its stomach. If you do not understand anything, telephone your breeder for advice. Your diet sheet and general information should also include the worming programme carried out and the procedure from now onwards.

Finally, before leaving your home to collect your puppy, ensure that all your fences and gates are secure and there are no little holes through which the puppy can escape.

Bringing your puppy home

Puppies are usually ready to leave the nest at seven to eight weeks. Before the big day arrives, make sure you have all the puppy needs in store for its food. Personally, I usually send puppies off with a starter pack so that they keep to the same food, and also prepare their next meat meal, so the new owner can see how it is served.

You will need two dog bowls, one for water and one for food. Stainless steel bowls are the most practical and hygienic, although you can buy plastic (chewable) or china (breakable). The puppy will need a bed of his own in his very own place where he can sleep undisturbed. I prefer the hard, fibreglass beds which are easy to clean and indestructable. An adult Golden will need the 30in (76cm) size, and you can buy a furry pad or blanket to fit, which is easily washable. There are many other types of bed: basketware, doggy duvets and bean bags, to name but a few. You will need a houndglove for the dog's daily grooming; velvet one side and wire on the reverse, together with a good quality steel comb. I prefer the type with a wooden handle. Later on, a chamois leather is useful to dry your Golden after walks, and also his own towel. A few toys should be bought for playtime and chewing: hard rubber dumb-bells, round rings, smoked bones, but never anything too small that could lodge in the puppy's throat and choke him. You will have checked your fences, but have you checked

Right: *Essential grooming equipment — brushes; hound glove; steel comb; serrated scissors for trimming; other scissors for tail and feet; nail clippers.*

electrical points and appliances?
Turn them off when not in use and
even put a wire shield around them
so that the puppy does not
electrocute himself!

All that remains now is to collect
your new companion. If you have a
young family, it would be wise to
avoid collection at the weekends
and time it for mid-week when they
are at school. The puppy will then
get plenty of rest and you can
establish a routine with him. The
children can enjoy the puppy on
coming home from school.

You should consider the puppy's
routine and avoid collection at meal
times. It is best to collect early in
the day and then he will have time
to settle before bedtime. Discuss
with your breeder your plans and
she or he will ensure that the
puppy's meals are adjusted so that
he is either fed earlier or waits till
you reach home, depending on
length of journey, so that he is not
sick. You should take a roll of paper

towel and old newspapers just in
case. I find puppies usually travel
best in the front passenger area
between your feet; they get more
air and do not move too much, but
you should line the floor with
paper.

On arrival home, take the puppy
out into the garden to relieve
himself and let him quietly discover
his new territory. If due for a feed
present it to the puppy. Let him
follow you into the house and
discover where he will sleep, his
toys and a little geography. Unless
you are with the puppy, limit this to
the kitchen where he cannot do
too much damage. Try to leave the
back door open so he can train
himself. At night, put newspaper
on the floor by the back door where
he will relieve himself. The
principles of toilet training are the
same as for a baby. When the
puppy wakes, let him out, and
again when he has eaten. They
train quickly, and many of mine are
clean when they leave home.

When bedtime comes, put the
puppy firmly in his bed with a
baby's rusk or a small biscuit, turn
out the light and leave him. The
puppy will be so exhausted he will

Below: *Suitable toys enjoyed by
Goldens — large, solid ball, firm
rubber ring, large squeaky toys and
smoked bones.*

21

fall asleep instantly. If it should wake up and whimper, resist the temptation or you will be forever having sleepless nights. Do make sure the children do not leave plastic toys around for the puppy to swallow or any other small objects. The puppy will grow at an alarming rate, so keep all countertops clear or you will lose food, knives, dishcloths, tea towels, oven gloves and any other such articles!

Remember the puppy is only eight weeks old and too much play will tire him and lead to over excitement and irritableness. Remember that he must be undisturbed when asleep. Do not play tug of war with him as this will damage his teeth. Do not allow the puppy to chew concrete, metal objects or stones; all things he will like to do with disastrous results to his teeth and internal organs. When you allow the puppy the privilege of your company in the lounge, make sure he knows where his place is to sit, and make him understand that it is a room for good behaviour, not games. Above all, remember he is a dog and does not need to sit on the sofa or sleep in your bed.

General care
Goldens are usually a very healthy breed and do not require much daily attention to maintain good health. You should be prepared to give the puppy a quick grooming daily with houndglove and comb. Once outside activities begin, if the puppy becomes muddy – and he will – hose him down on returning home, dry with a towel and finally with the chamois.

His ears should be cleaned regularly every week with pet wipes. If you feel they are excessively brown and waxy, get some drops from the veterinarian. It is always a good plan to keep first-aid remedies in the house such as eye and ear drops. If they bother the dog excessively, ie if he shakes his head or scratches, a visit to the veterinarian is in order. The puppy's nails should be trimmed regularly with nail clippers, back to the 'quick' – the soft, fleshy area inside the nail. But be careful not to cut into this part of the nail.

At about four to four and a half months, the puppy will begin his second teething and his milk teeth will begin to drop out, but this does not usually worry the Golden excessively. The puppy may have sore gums and go off his biscuits. The main area of concern I would draw your attention to is if the milk

Below: *Well-shaped feet rarely need nail clipping, nor Goldens that walk correctly and have road exercise.*

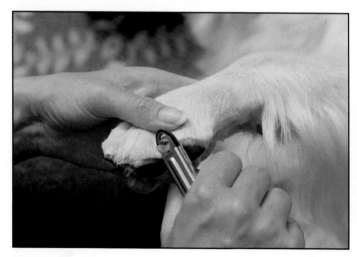

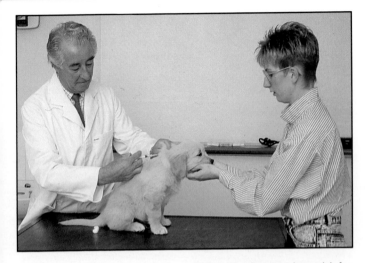

Above: *The first veterinary visit for inoculations establishes friendly relations between your veterinarian and dog for life.*

teeth are tenacious and do not drop out, so check regularly. If the permanent teeth grow through on the outside of the milk teeth, you may have problems. The first thing to do is to give a hefty marrow bone which may dislodge the baby teeth. If this does not work, you must pay a visit to the veterinarian and have the baby teeth removed. Otherwise your puppy could develop a bad mouth. A good idea after this is to feed the puppy with a bowl on a step where it has to reach up and over for its food. This may encourage a good bite.

Inoculations

Inoculations can start at eight or nine weeks of age, with a second vaccination being given at 12 weeks old. Using modern vaccines this will give protection by 13 weeks of age and your puppy will be inoculated against Distemper, Hepatitis, Leptospirosis, Parvo-virus and Parainfluenza. The precise instructions for each vaccine should be confirmed with your veterinary surgeon at the initial appointment.

After the initial course of vaccinations, your pup will require an annual booster. Your vet should send you a reminder card, but make a note of the due date anyway so there is no danger of these vital shots being missed.

Very often the visit to the vet for these initial inoculations will be your pup's first experience of such things so try to make it as fun and relaxing as possible for him. Any bad experience will be remembered as will a good experience. My dogs all seem to enjoy going to the vet for whatever reason.

Training your puppy

Puppies, like children, respond well to discipline and are happier for it. Keep it simple. Voice control is effective by tone and strength. Limit the vocabulary to simple commands with hand definition where appropriate. Goldens are very biddable and really only want to please, once they know what you want. One of your first tasks is to ensure the puppy knows that you may remove his dog bowl and he will receive it back, likewise with a bone or a toy. You must establish that you are the boss and the puppy is a lesser being. He must know that any attempt at protest or rebellion will bring a smart tap on the nose with your fingers. A sharp scolding is usually enough to send a Golden into a nervous breakdown, so it is not difficult to have the upper hand. It you should have a more assertive puppy, trying to dominate as he gets older, pick him up by the scruff of the neck and shake him at the same time scolding. Puppies should not be left alone for too long, and even as adults for not more than four hours. If you are going to leave a puppy to go shopping it is best to feed, play and then he will sleep in your absence. He must certainly be taught solitude at some time or you will lead a very restricted life.

Sometimes it is a good idea to have a small shed and wired dog run where you can put the dog on certain occasions, such as gardening, a children's party, when you are vacuum cleaning or doing a lot of cooking. Always leave the puppy with his toys; he must be happy there.

It is also good to invest in a horn whistle from a gunshop. On a windy day it is not much good yelling 'Fido', and to get the puppy to act on a whistle is a practical exercise: one blast for sit and stay, three sharp pips for come quick. If accompanied by charade-like gestures overacted to the extreme, he should soon get the message.

Exercise for the puppy

The first thing every new owner appears to want to do is take their new puppy out and show him off! Fortunately, the new pattern of injections precludes this since the puppy cannot go out until after the programme is completed. In this matter seek your veterinarian's advice, since in some rural areas where there have not been any recent outbreaks of canine diseases he or she may relax the rule to allow you to socialize and familiarize the puppy with cars etc, just outside your own home after

the second injection. However, there is nothing to prevent your puppy getting used to car rides and visiting relatives or friends, providing any pets they own have been fully booster-injected, and provided you carry the puppy and do not let him walk on alien ground.

Golden Retriever puppies really do not need masses of exercise and the pattern of exercise must be carefully studied and monitored. Their bones are soft and not finally settled in their sockets until two years-old, so you have to be very careful. Whilst all dogs like a good scamper, lead walking can be more beneficial, especially in their first year and certainly in the first six months. Since you cannot take the puppy out very early, you will have to do your preliminary lead training in the garden. A good romp in the garden will be sufficient to tire him

out and his energies can be directed to retrieving his toys to hand.

When, at around four months, the puppy takes his first outing, do not make it too long since he will find all the new noises and distractions quite exhausting. About a ¼ to ½ mile (40-80m) will be sufficient and you may not even rise to that amount! At about five to six months go further afield to a park, a common or woods. When you watch the puppy moving away from you and his back legs appear stronger — as if they belong to his body and not wobbly — then let him have a short, free run but it is most important that this takes place on absolutely firm, even ground where he cannot trip down holes.

From seven to eight months, the puppy can do more extensive walks and free running, but never too far to overtire him, having previously ascertained that he will return on call. A bribe can be quite useful. Remember he is covering much more ground than you. My adult males usually have a five-mile (8-km) jog in the forest or a six-mile (9.7km) road walk but not until late adolescence, say at about 18 months to two years. Remember if you give a Golden a mile, he will be ready for two miles a day. If you gave him ten he would want twenty! So ensure that you keep your Golden to the amount of exercise which keeps him fit and for which you have time and energy.

I think it is a mistake to make the exercise regularly at certain times of the day. There will always be some time when a family crisis or some other activity must take precedence, and then you have a discontented dog. Surprise him with a walk, so that he thinks 'Oh great, we're off', rather than the time coming round for his usual walk and for some reason you cannot go, and then he is sulking, saying 'When are we going?'

Left: *The puppies' first taste of freedom — exploring the garden which, to them, is a jungle of new adventures.*

Diet

Follow your breeder's diet sheet to the letter. It is quite likely with distractions of new friends, a family of his own and so much freedom that the puppy may not be very interested in his meals. After three to four days he will adjust and get back to normal. If there are any problems, contact the puppy's breeder and seek advice. If you wish to alter anything or feel he needs different food, again contact the breeder and seek more advice.

For those of you who have not purchased from a breeder and may not have been given a full diet sheet, I present here the diet my eight-week puppies consume.

As your Golden grows up, you will turn to some other food. The variety is enormous: fresh meat, frozen meat, canned meat, dried all-in-one foods, dry flakes, mixers, terrier meals, small biscuit, very large biscuits. So it is up to you to decide which type of feeding fits your lifestyle, and which is your Golden's choice. I personally favour a natural diet of meat in some form and 50 per cent carbohydrate, but as the Golden will eagerly snap up any family leftovers, you may find you have to reduce the latter.

Below: *My recommended diet sheet for an eight-week old Golden.*

Diet for an eight-week old puppy	
9 am	170g (6oz) lean raw chopped beef and 30ml (2 tablespoons) of mixer (kibble/biscuit) with a vitamin/mineral supplement, given as instructed on container.
2 pm	250ml (½ pint/10 fl oz) goat's milk (or evaporated milk diluted as instructions on can) together with a wholewheat cereal flaky biscuit rusk, thickened with baby cereal, or with a baby rusk to chew.
6 pm	As 9 am feed without vitamin/mineral supplement.
10 pm	As 2 pm feed.

Increase meat allowance by 28g (1oz) each week and increase mixer (kibble/biscuit), which you feed dry, until puppy is having 453g (1lb) meat and about 226g (8oz) mixer (kibble), together with his 0.5 litre (1 UK pint) milk and cereal.

Be careful giving cow's milk since it can cause upsets. At three months meals may be separated into three with the same quantities. At six months reduce to two meals daily. Rice pudding or custard can be given as part of the milk ration. After nine months he may prefer only one meal daily, but better growth is maintained with two.

Car travel

Some puppies travel well, some not so well. Whichever category your puppy falls into, introduce him immediately to short journeys in the car. It is most important to prevent them rolling and climbing around which induces sickness. Obviously an estate (station wagon) or hatchback is more practical. If an estate car, you should invest in a dog guard. You should put a blanket, woolly bed or a doggy duvet on the floor so he has a firm grip whether sitting up or lying down. Lift the puppy out of the car so that he does not jar his shoulders and hurt himself.

Take a short journey every day, perhaps to collect the children from

Above: *At peace with the world: full up with food, worn out from his adventures and dreaming of more to come.*

school. When he is allowed out take the puppy a little further and end it with a nice walk. Even if he is sick, keep persevering — they rarely feel really ill. By this time make sure he knows that he must not get out of the car until told to. He must learn to stay until called.

If taking a long journey, children's anti sea-sickness pills may ease the trauma. Give one the night before and one an hour before setting off; and they do not make the dog sleepy. Do not feed before any journey, short or long. If you have a saloon car the back seat can give a bumpy ride and the well of the front passenger seat gives a more secure ride. Once you know the puppy is no longer sick, you can transfer him to the back seat.

Socialization

Once the final inoculations are over, the dog's real life will begin. Familiarize him with multiple experiences. Take him to meet the children from school. Shopping in a busy street is a valuable experience — traffic, bikes, pushchairs and those terrible shopping bags on wheels. Make the puppy respect cats — no chasing here. Usually the cat is boss.

If you live in the country, get him used to horses, cattle, sheep, ducks, chickens — everything that makes up your rural life. Deer and game are very exciting but I am afraid you will not contain this except by being aware ahead of the puppy and putting him on the lead.

Let him meet other breeds of dog and learn to be sociable and friendly with them. Take him to a ringcraft class. Golden Retriever Breed Clubs run friendly classes, usually once a month, in many areas, and these are social occasions for both owners and dogs.

Responsibility to the general public

One of the laws of dog ownership

is that dogs must wear a collar with an address tag attached. Do not put the dog's name, just your own surname, address and telephone number. Dogs are stolen not only from home but also on walks, and it gives thieves a disctinct advantage to know the pet's name.

Always carry a plastic bag in your pocket and if your dog fouls the park or street, clear it up with this and dispose. Just pick up with the bag and reverse it so that all the excrement is contained.

Make sure your dog walks nicely on its new collar and lead. Rather than buying expensive leather equipment, invest in either a smartly-coloured nylon collar and lead (they are very strong) or a canvas collar with leather ends and lead to match. Your Golden will enjoy water and revel in muddy pools, and this equipment is easily washed. Keep the puppy under control and do not let him jump up at people.

Everyone admires a good-looking, friendly and well-behaved dog but if uncontrollable he can be a perfect pest. Attention to early training and a friendly firm hand in his first year of life will pay dividends for the future.

Below: *A typical Golden ringcraft class, incorporating handling, socialization and trimming demonstrations.*

29

Chapter Three

EVERYDAY TRAINING

We have touched on early training when you first bring your puppy home. Now we will recap and add to your knowledge. Go slowly — do not confuse your dog with too much information. Keep each lesson short so he does not get bored or lose his concentration. Do not get cross if he does not immediately understand what you expect from him — this is probably because you are not too good as a teacher. Be patient and try again, and go over the top on praise at each little achievement.

Toilet training

The immediate priority will be toilet training. Most puppies do not like to soil their bed or homes and if a door is open will step outside to be clean. When they wake up, when they have eaten, when they start panting and going round in circles sniffing for a place, then point them in the right direction. Improve on this gradually by escorting them to the place you would prefer them to desecrate! Then they will gradually learn to return to that place. Praise lavishly once this is achieved.

Early training

Next the puppy has to appreciate the hierarchy. You are number one chief and he is merely one of the Indians! You are the provider of all that is wonderful in life: food, walks, toys, cuddles, games, a comfortable home and a good bed. He must realize never to step out of line as you will not tolerate this. Goldens are a gentle, biddable breed and very easily trained. But do not think they will not try to get their own way early in life. Make sure they know they stand corrected in no uncertain way. Usually a stern scolding is enough and lessons repeated until understood.

The dog must know that you present him with a bowl of food and may also take it away at any time. He must respect this and have the confidence that it will be returned. If he objects, scold severely and lightly tap him on the nose. Naughty boy or girl is a lesson to be learned as well as good boy or girl. The dog will soon know which he prefers. This lesson must be learnt with all the things you share: toys, bones, sticks, dummies — they must be shared not possessed. We have a young Rottweiler in our family and if you hold a biscuit between your teeth she takes it so gently you do not know it, and my champion stud dog was just the same. This gives a terrific rapport between you both — absolute trust.

Basic commands

Now you understand one another better, we will proceed to commands which require concentration. First you want the

Above: *A lesson that must be learnt well and remembered forever — food bowl, toys etc must be shared not possessed.*

dog to 'come' and a good way to demand this is to prepare his food, walk away with it and call 'Come Sandy' at the same time urging him forward with a wave of your hand. Praise every time, and when this word is learnt, use it on other occasions as well. Another lesson to be learned is 'back' accompanied by a hand thrust backwards to emphasize what is required. This command is very important to the dog's life. If you open a door or gate, he must not rush out — it could be in front of a car. When you open the car tail-gate, the same

31

command applies — you could be about to mend a puncture on a busy road and the dog might jump out to his death.

The obvious follow-up to 'back' is 'stay' and both these commands should be delivered in a stern, heavy voice which indicates you mean the dog to obey, not a weak voice which indicates you hope he will! Accompany the command with your hand held high. The fourth command is 'no' and 'leave' with a hand signal pointing at the dog. Be consistent with your commands and signals; do not vary them or integrate them. Keep your vocabulary short and consistent, then you will get results. Also use your voice tone to indicate your meaning. This is a further indication to your puppy of what is expected of him. Be lavish with the praise.

Manners in the home

Having succeeded with basic obedience commands, we turn to behaviour in the home. The dog should not be allowed to prance up and down the stairs. To emphasize this, put a baby gate across the base. Firstly there could be an accident if he decides to pelt down the stairs knocking you down. Secondly, it will do the puppy's front no good, making his front legs

Right: *Another command to be thoroughly learnt, which is vital to your dog's life: stay back when gates are opened.*

Below: *The command 'stay' is most important; you must be confident your dog will stay on opening the car tailgate.*

Above: *There are many new types of collars and leads to check boisterous dogs. Here you see the halter in use.*

Below: *A well-trained Golden enjoying a companionable walk on the lead. The initial time and effort is well worthwhile.*

wide apart and out at elbow. When allowed to sit with you in the lounge in the evening, he must appreciate that this is a privilege only gained by extremely good behaviour. A dog who keeps pacing around or playing interferes with your evening — that behaviour should be confined to the kitchen or garden.

'Manners' is the next word to teach and accompany this command by placing the dog firmly on a rug or mat or in a corner of the room and tell him to 'stay'. In fact 'manners' is one of my most useful words at other times as well. The dog will soon learn that if he has no 'manners' then he must leave the room!

At all times, chat away to your puppy as a companion. He will learn a lot from the tone of your voice and will soon appreciate house routine. One of my little bitches could run the household single-handed, so well-tuned is she to the order and timing of events! If your puppy is constantly jumping up at you, one possible way of discouraging is to raise your knee to his chest and push him down shouting 'off'.

Outside training
Now to outside activities and training. Referring back to our puppy chapter, socialize your young dog in every direction and with every object or animal you may encounter. Teach him to walk on the lead without pulling. Check chains are useful in this training if used correctly. Allow plenty of slack, so if he pulls you can jerk the dog up sharply with plenty of chain in hand. Likewise, flexible leads and halters are very useful. Teach him to 'heel', pointing behind you and slapping your side. Do not allow the dog to be loose until you have ensured he will 'come'. Use the whistle, one long blast to 'stay' and three sharp quick bursts to return at the double. Keep your eyes open when exercising for diversions which will encourage him to disobey you. Also look out for other dogs which may threaten to harm your dog or destroy his confidence.

Whilst not restricting his exercise, do not let your dog amble about with unlimited freedom. Make your walks companionable. I always feel sorry for dogs let out on their own for exercise. They look so lonely. Every now and again, call him to heel and do a little training. Teach your dog to fetch and retrieve. Teach him to sit to heel and stay. Then throw either a stick or a canvas dummy a short way. Tell him to wait and restrain him by hand at first. Then send him in to fetch and bring the stick or dummy back to you, and eventually to sit and put it in your hand. Again, this deserves lavish praise. Keep the lessons brief. Never make your dog bored and always finish on a successful high.

A well-trained dog is a joy to own, and if you should decide to own two then the second will also be well trained by your first Golden.

Chapter Four

THE ADULT GOLDEN RETRIEVER

Feeding

Feeding all depends on what suits your lifestyle and the health of your dog. It also depends on the age of your dog and his activities. I prefer a natural diet, although there are plenty of excellent complete feeds on the market. The manufacturer's instructions should always be followed carefully when feeding complete feeds. Males and females needs are very different. The young adult male is a scrawny adolescent whereas the bitches soon tend to be overweight.

Generally, I feed protein in some form, be it fresh meat, tripe (organ meats), or canned food and blend 50 per cent carbohydrate into this. The latter can vary tremendcusly from biscuit meal, mixer (kibble), bread, pasta or whatever they like. This is the main principle; let us now consider specific cases.

Let us consider the males first. They are much livelier than bitches and burn their food off at an alarming rate. Like a teenage son, they are always hungry. They benefit more from two meals daily than one. Between a year and two years they seem to need as much as you can pump into them, anything from 780-907g (1½-2lb) meat, lots of pasta and mixer, and even an all-in-one food for the second meal, naturally combined with exercise. They seem to crave more of the latter than the girls.

If a young dog is used at stud, or is holidaying with the family and walking long distances, just keep pumping the food in. Once the dog begins to leave food, cut his rations down. Eventually he will develop into a well-bodied animal without excess weight and then you can establish his diet to probably 453g (1lb) meat and some form of carbohydrate. Remember to take into account the amount of exercise the dog takes. It is important to keep a close eye on exercise and diet to maintain a healthy dog.

Now for the bitches – they are absolute pigs. In fact *all* Goldens are, given the opportunity. Most bitches do not need as much food as the males. Once fully grown they can probably do with a handful of biscuits or mixer (kibble) and 340g (12oz) of meat. Again, if working or having extensive exercise it can be increased slightly, but with their season and hormones they tend to flab just like us human females! Once the fat is there, it is difficult to remove.

Remember, when dogs lose coat, they also lose all rib and body. Do not be fooled and feed them up. It is essential to imagine them with the coat on top, since when they return to full coat they will look quite unsightly if you have increased their food.

Obesity

If you suddenly find your Golden is overweight, all is not lost. You will have to exercise him more and free running is not the answer since it builds up muscle on the shoulders and once that is there you will not shift it. You can strictly control the diet and combine with exercise, cutting out all carbohydrates and feeding only protein and vitamin additives. They really can live off their fat for two to three weeks! You can alternate this regime with canned 'obesity diet' from your veterinarian, not giving the stated ration or they will continue to increase — half a can one day and three-quarters the next. There are also low-calorie dry foods available that produce excellent results. In fact, the Golden can rarely find room for the full ration allowed!

Do not decide that your dog needs a variety of foods. Once you have found the food that suits your dog, stick to it. If you feed scraps from the table, weigh them and make it part of their daily ration. Always weigh meals since you can be deceived by the meal dish. When feeding fresh meat, I feed it raw, but be governed by the dog's preference.

The older dog

The oldies become very special and indeed get a new lease of life around nine years young. If their usual food still suits their stomachs and digestion, on no account change it. Variety could be their downfall. If they do ail with liver or kidney problems, they may well turn to a chicken or fish diet, or even a convalescent diet from your veterinarian. But while all is well do not interfere.

Keep their exercise going as long as you can — it keeps life's interest up. They will eventually have good and bad days, so bear with them. Sometimes they will want a longer walk, sometimes a very short one and some days none at all. Let them have a corner where they can watch the household and family activities without worry. Let them have the privileges of old age; give them a soft bed to rest their limbs.

Below: *A lovely quality Golden out of coat. Condition is lost with the coat, but will return with the coat, so do not feed up.*

Old dogs can be either overweight, sometimes tending to dropsy, but more likely they will get too thin. Try not to let this happen since too soon the back end wastes away and their back legs become too weak.

Finally, when the time comes and you wonder whether to or whether not, measure up the quality of your dog's life and perhaps your own selfishness in wishing to prolong it, and let him have a dignified end, having enjoyed his life to the full. When the time comes you will know in your heart what to do.

Grooming

Regular attention to grooming will keep both your dog and your home tidier. Basically, you will need a houndglove, a mitten which has short wire on one side and a velvet polisher on the reverse. You groom with the wire and then polish his coat with the other side. A good quality steel comb with fine teeth and preferably a wooden handle is also essential. You should also have

Above: *An older Golden in comfort on a soft rug. Make sure your oldies can enjoy the privileges of old age.*

a chamois leather to dry him after exercise and of course his own towel. A daily grooming takes only a few minutes but is essential when the dog casts its coat, since it comes out in large handfuls. You should also invest in some nail clippers, good quality thinning scissors and some straight scissors. Well-shaped feet that are exercised on hard ground do not often need the nails trimming, unless the dog walks incorrectly and then nails grow too long.

Thinning scissors are to keep the Golden's neck and front tidy. Trim underneath the coat so that the top remains long — your aim in thinning is to tidy if a pet, but if a show dog to enhance its good points. All the Breed Clubs hold regular trimming sessions to help you. It is well worth a visit to one of these since your Golden will look better and not scatter so much mud over your home. The straight scissors are to trim his tail. Take the tail in your left hand and find the end bone. Trim half an inch (1.3cm) beyond and in a fan shape leaving about 4in (10cm) of feathering. These scissors are also for keeping the shape of the foot tidy. Trim excess hair from the foot following its shape and take out all the clumps and tufts of hair in the centre, between the pads. The dog will then be able to walk more comfortably. Also trim round the shape of the ears with the thinning scissors to keep them looking tidy. See Chapter Seven for photographs of a trimming session.

One of the best times to give a full trimming session is when your Golden has been completely out of coat and the hair is beginning to grow. This will enable you to get the shape before too much coat grows in, and a weekly tidy-up will produce a wonderful result when the dog is in full coat. Never trim savagely. Do a little and wait till the next day and take a long look and assess how much more you need to take off. The thinning scissors should have fine teeth so that scissor marks never show.

General care

Care of the adult Golden is fairly straightforward. Whilst grooming you should examine the coat to make sure it is not harbouring any parasites such as fleas. It is difficult to detect lice, but if your dog is constantly scratching and licking, producing a pink tummy, it is as well to give a suitable insecticidal bath shampoo, obtainable on advice from your veterinarian. A soothing rinse powder made up with water will also help. Another cause of irritation can be squirrel mites, ants and mosquitoes. Particularly in summer it is wise to give regular baths to reduce parasite risk and to cool the skin.

Also whilst grooming you should inspect the ears at least twice-weekly to make sure they are free from mites or brown wax. Wet

eczema in the ears may not be visible one day but make a dramatic appearance the following morning (see Chapter Five).

Eyes should also be kept healthy and any discharge wiped away. Pet wipes are very useful, but veterinary advice should be sought if the discharge continues.

Any pus discharge from either the penis or vulva should also be dealt with immediately by the veterinarian.

General care involves detailed inspections daily so that you know immediately if anything has developed, ensuring the greatest chance of a high recovery rate.

Worming

Puppies are wormed regularly as explained earlier and adult dogs should be wormed every three months to ensure that they are kept free of infestation. Worming preparations are readily available from your veterinary surgeon and he or she will be able to advise which one is best suited to your dog, whether it be a powder, a course of tablets etc. Wormers can also be bought from pet supply shops and these treatments can be effective provided that the manufacturer's instructions are followed carefully.

Among the many endoparasites which can infect a dog are roundworms (Toxocara canis and Toxascaris leonina), and tapeworms (Dipyldium caninum). A routine worming program will prevent infestation.

In recent years, there has been much publicity over the Toxocara canis larvae reaching the retina of the eye in humans and subsequently damaging the vision or even leading to the loss of the affected eye. This is a rare occurrence and, providing your dog is wormed regularly, this should not be a cause of concern.

In some countries, such as the United States of America and Australia, heartworm is quite a problem since this can be fatal. It is transmitted by mosquitoes and requires a daily preventative pill dose. Your veterinarian should be consulted.

Chapter Five

HEALTH PROBLEMS

It is essential to make your puppy's visits to the veterinarian happy events and to help establish a rapport and faith between the two. The dog must learn that the vet is his best friend (next to you) and will always help him if in trouble. Try to make his first visit and introduction a good one. Do not sit around a crowded waiting room waiting to catch kennel cough or some other disease. Leave the dog in the car until it is his turn.

Giving pills

Take a firm approach when you have to give your dog pills. Open his mouth and put the pill right down the back of the throat. Close the mouth and rub his larynx swiftly so that he swallows. There is really no need for bits of meat and butter to encase the pill. If you tackle the job from the start with purpose, your dog will always accept his medicine. Some dogs I have had accept them as a sweetmeat — a great treat!

Inoculations

Naturally, one of your dog's first visits, or *the* first visit, will be to

Below: *The veterinarian examines a puppy for hernia and other abnormalities.*

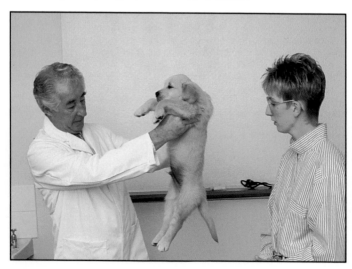

protect him from Distemper, Hardpad, Leptospirosis, Hepatitis and Canine Parvo-virus. It is hard to make the puppy happy when a needle is thrust into his skin! But with a good veterinarian, he will feel very little. Give a titbit reward for good behaviour. Ask your vet for the up-to-date programme for these inoculations since they do alter from time to time. Usually, the first Distemper injection is given at nine weeks, the second and first Parvo-virus at 12 weeks and the last Parvo at 18 weeks. It is important that they are not done too soon because if the mother has a very high immunity to these diseases, then her puppy may also have this high immunity and the inoculation will have no effect, leaving the puppy totally unprotected.

It is important to have annual boosters. It is a sad fact that whereas the Distemper plus three injections fully protects, the Parvo injections do not fully protect in as much as the dog can still contract the disease but probably to a lesser degree. It really is a killer and the dreadful stench of the sickness and diarrhoea is never to be forgotten.

Immediate attention is necessary as dehydration is rapid and a healthy dog will become a shell within hours.

Ears
Ears should be inspected regularly for wax, ear mites and wet eczema (see over). Keep them clean by using proprietary pet wipes designed for this purpose and if in trouble seek veterinary advice. It is advisable to keep ear drops in the first-aid cupboard, but only those supplied by your veterinarian.

Eyes
At certain times of the year, conjunctivitis can be quite prevalent. Again, seek veterinary advice. The eyes look sore and sometimes there is a white discharge; eye drops will soon put this right. Again, it is wise to keep some in the first-aid cupboard since the condition may occur over a weekend when advice is not readily

Below: *An adult Golden undergoing a routine health check together with an examination of infected ears.*

41

to hand. Some eye ointments and drops should *not* be used once they have been open for more than one month. I really do believe that dogs can be victims of the high pollen count, as humans can be, and to allergies which can cause discharge from the eyes.

Eczema

There are two types of eczema — wet and dry. Most cases of eczema are self-inflicted and treatable by simple remedies. Whatever the cause, the dog starts to nibble, scratch and lick, resulting in a patch of eczema. It can be caused by fleas, mosquito bites, dry skin, or even allergies to wheat or carpet fibre which can cause the itch. Initially, ease the hair away from the wound so that it does not stick to the skin and cleanse the wound with a weak, non-toxic disinfectant solution or just salt water. Dry with a clean towel. Probably the most effective remedy is to dab with neat antiseptic fluid which will dry it up within 24 hours. Another is to use a selenium sulphide-based shampoo from the veterinarian, not as a shampoo but to dab neat onto the wound, having first cleansed the wound, as I have already described. Leave for 30 seconds before washing off the shampoo and drying with a towel. Repeat several times a day and you should have good results within 36 hours. Another good remedy is a calomine-based ointment which is very soothing. Anti-histamine pills will stop the itching. If the problem persists after two or three days, contact your veterinarian for an injection to ease the irritation.

It is a good idea to keep a plastic ('Elizabethan') collar from the vet. If your dog wears this, it will not be able to continue licking and scratching the offending part! You may think that your dog would not wear the collar and that you would not, in any case, subject it to such an indignity, but wearing the collar is infinitely preferable to the irritation. My dogs wear the 'bonnet', as we call it, happily and it comes off for walks. It is also

wise to bath your Golden in an anti-parasite shampoo, but some skins are very sensitive to these shampoos. It also helps to put a spoonful of cooking oil in their dinner. Dry skin itches and it is good to get oil inside the dog to provide the hair with oil to prevent the dryness.

Enzyme deficiency

If your dog does not benefit from his food, has loose motions, sickness with undigested food and

Right: *Checking teeth; first teeth are sometimes retained and must be removed to ensure adult teeth have the correct bite.*

Below: *The veterinarian examines the puppy's chest with a stethoscope for heart and breathing problems.*

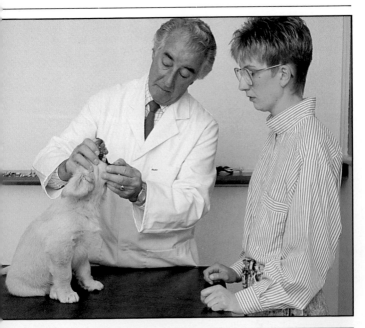

generally fails to 'body-up', do take a sample of faeces to your veterinarian as your dog may well have a pancreas deficiency. The condition is controllable and veterinary advice must be sought as soon as possible.

Cancer

Nearly all breeds suffer from some form of cancer these days, from youth to old age. My own experience has been that the disease has developed very rapidly and within a short time. I have saved my dogs pain and suffering by making the painful decision to have the veterinarian end their lives. They have lived their lives to the full until that point.

Always watch your dog carefully – his eyes are a good guide to pain or suffering – and it is essential that when you notice something unusual to contact your veterinarian. The earlier you spot a problem and give your veterinarian a complete outline, the sooner a diagnosis can be made and the relevant treatment given. This gives your dog the greatest chance to achieve full recovery.

Hereditary defects

The breeders of Golden Retrievers accept that there are hereditary defects in the breed, but not that they have necessarily been proved to be completely so. However, we take advice from the specialists and do try to eradicate these from the Golden. We can only do the best we can, but it does not mean that if we follow all the specialists advice, we can eliminate these faults completely from the breed.

Hip dysplasia Ideally *all* dogs should be X-rayed and scored from the age of 12 months by the BVA. This would help the breeders to know what they are producing. If ten puppies are born and only two X-rayed and scored, it is not a good indication of results on the whole litter. Of course, X-raying all dogs would be the ideal procedure but unfortunately, in practise, this is difficult to achieve.

However, *all* breeding stock, male and female, must be X-rayed and scored. Each hip is scored 0-53. The ideal would be 0-0, which is not very often achieved; the high scores are very bad. It is advisable to score good and bad hips so that our breed average is accurate. If only good hips are submitted, it would give a false picture. In the UK, the breed average has remained pretty steady over the years. At the time of writing it is 20. But up-to-date information will be obtainable from the Breed Club Secretaries. In the UK, these Secretaries receive regular reports from Dr. Malcolm Willis, our geneticist.

Hip Dysplasia means that the hip joint is badly formed with perhaps a shallow joint (acetabulum), or the femoral head may be misshapen. This could cause pain and arthritis later on, but I would emphasize that even Goldens with good hips, as working dogs out in all weathers, can still develop arthritis. The really critical hip cases often occur between six and nine months when the puppy becomes uncomfortably in pain on getting up and down, very stiff and later very lame. Eventually it will whimper at the pain. These are usually the operable cases and there are several operations now available to alleviate the condition and expert advice must be sought.

Those dogs who do not have super hips may well live normal lives without inconvenience. My first pet Golden was eight when he suddenly could not rise from the lawn. On X-ray, he had no sockets at all and in those days had a series of gold injections. He then lived to 14 years without discomfort and his

Above right: *A veterinarian examining a young puppy for soundness and hopefully no early signs of hip dysplasia.*

Right: *Checking temperature; a rise can indicate infection. It is a good idea to learn how to do this yourself.*

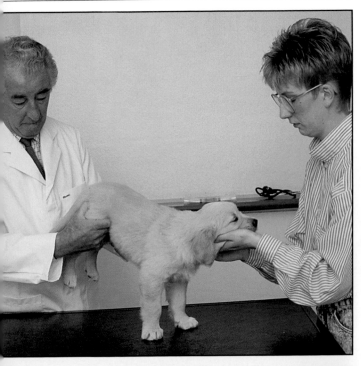

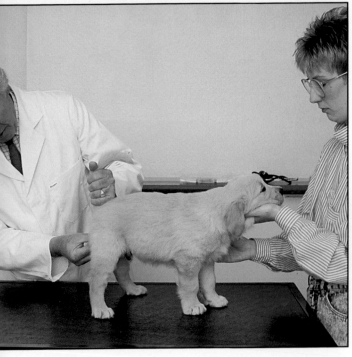

back legs moved like pistons. He then died of a bad heart!

Get the subject in perspective. Dr Willis tells us temperament first, breed-type second, eye diseases next and hips after that. It is quite possible for poor hips to breed good when put to a dog that produces good hips. It is also possible for a perfect hip scorer to produce very poor hips or some dogs with average hips.

Hereditary cataract   Again, it would be ideal if all puppies were examined for this condition after one year of age annually, to give us a true record of what breeders are producing. Unfortunately, only those dogs which are shown or bred from regularly have their eyes checked, and there is no knowledge of the other litter mates. Also unfortunately, in the past the Kennel Club in London and the British Veterinary Association have only kept records of the passes and not the failures. In Britain, the eye examination must be undertaken by one of the panel of opthalmic specialists appointed by the BVA. They should be examined every year of their lives. Affected animals should not be bred from but only two per cent of affected Goldens actually lose their sight.

Goldens can develop cataract at any stage of their life and they are a

breed that has late-developing cataracts, at seven years or even ten years-old, by which time they could have produced or sired many puppies. We are told that clear parents do not produce cataract but this has been proven wrong many times, although the parents could perhaps be late developers.

PRA This is Progressive Retinal Atrophy, sometimes referred to as 'night blindness'. Some twenty years ago, this was quite a problem but these days it is rarely found in Goldens. However, when you have the cataract examinations the eye specialist will also test for PRA at the same time.

Entropion (or inturning eyelids) Some twenty years ago, this condition was widespread in Golden puppies but is rarely seen in present times. It is believed to be a hereditary condition and is probably the one most easily corrected without hurt to the puppy. Affected dogs should not be bred from nor shown. The condition usually occurs between 5 weeks to 4 months and very often in strong headed puppies. The bottom eyelids (and in extreme cases the top also) turn inwards and the lashes scratch the eye and can cause ulceration. Surgery has to be undergone and it is critical that it be undertaken at exactly the right stage of head development so that the smallest scar results.

Osteochrondosis This is an orthopaedic condition, the cause of which has not yet been satisfactorily established. It occurs in the shoulder, elbow, hock or stifle joints particularly in the growing puppy period. It seems to afflict puppies who make a sudden, large growth in a short period. Bits of cartilage break and flake off causing acute pain; surgery is usually required to remove the errant pieces. Should your dog develop any form of lameness, you should seek investigative treatment from your veterinarian. Falling down holes on exercise and jumping from a high-backed car could also induce the condition. I cannot stress too strongly that you should not over exercise your puppy until the bones have fully developed, ie up to two years-old. Complete rest and immobilization is essential, even if a cage or sedation has to be used to implement rest. Very careful and gradual remedial exercise has to be organized over a very long period for eventual soundness.

Below: *A breeder with the veterinarian who has given health checks to mother and son and found them clear of problems.*

Chapter Six

BREEDING YOUR GOLDEN RETRIEVER

To breed or not to breed

In Britain, the Golden Retriever Breed Clubs' Rescue Officers nationwide rescue and rehome many Goldens each year.

What has this to do with breeding you ask? Goldens are too popular for their own good. Too many bitches are bred from indiscriminately, without thought to soundness, temperament, type and compatible pedigree. Too many puppies are born and not enough care taken in placing them in suitable homes, and indeed some of the novice breeders do not have sufficient knowledge for the task. This is the road to rescue.

Why do you want to breed from your bitch? Is she your much-loved pet and would you like a daughter from her? Goldens produce anything up to 14 puppies – although seven is the average. But should she produce ten, have you homes for the remaining nine puppies? Have you had her hips scored and do you have up-to-date eye certificates for hereditary cataract and PRA? Is she sound enough for breeding both physically, mentally and in temperament? Have you taken advice from more experienced breeders, or in particular from the breeder of your own Golden, if this was your source of purchase? Do they consider she has any major constructional faults and do they consider she has anything to offer

the breed? Do you feel justified in putting your much-loved Golden at risk because, contrary to generalization, not all bitches whelp easily or make good mothers? Supposing you were involved in extremely heavy veterinary fees

during this period, could you afford them? Indeed, have you enough money in the bank to feed ten puppies? At seven weeks, this could amount to ten pints (12½ US pints; 5.7 litres) of milk a day and some 8lbs (3.6kg) of meat. Can you afford to feed mother the first four weeks when she is pouring milk into the puppies? True, some of this money will be returned when the puppies are sold, but at the end of the day there will not be a great financial profit. Do you want a holiday or a new piece of furniture on the proceeds? Or do you really want the joy of rearing a litter?

Preparation for breeding

The first thing to do is make an appointment to have your bitch's eyes examined by an official eye specialist. Either ask your veterinarian or your nearest Breed Club Secretary for the name and telephone number of the nearest

specialist. In Britain, you must take along your bitch's registration certificate so that the specialist can stamp it and he or she will also issue a certificate to state pass or fail, for hereditary cataract and PRA. The more expensive test is to come, and this is why I advise having your bitch's eyes examined first, because if your bitch fails there is no point in spending money on a hip X-ray and score.

Find out if your veterinarian has X-ray equipment and ask some of the breeders where they have their X-rays done; there are good radiologists and some not so good

Below: *The superb results of selective breeding. Two famous kennels own five present-day title holders (see page 51): Gill and Philpott's Westley Samuel, Martha, Mabella, Jacob and Standerwick Thomasina.*

and the quality of your X-ray is important to the final hip score. Most breeders have a short list of the best. Hips are scored 0-53 on each leg and the lower the score the better. You should breed somewhere beneath the breed average and Breed Clubs receive regular reports from the geneticist on these statistics. A telephone call to your Breed Club Secretary will give you up-to-date information.

The right time to breed

Ideally I like to breed on a bitch's second season. However, all things are variable and we have to take into consideration how often she comes into season. If this is at six-month intervals, you would not mate before the third season. If this is eight or nine months, then the second season would be satisfactory. Again, we have to take into account the temperament of the young bitch. Is she a baby and should be left until older or is she a settled nature and more likely to be motherly. *Do not* leave it until she is four or five years, as some people do, and suddenly decide they must have a puppy from her or it will do her good to have a litter! By this time she will be so humanized that she will more than likely reject a male, and if a forced mating is

achieved she is unlikely to take too kindly to a box full of puppies. In considering the 'right' time, work out carefully when the babies are due. When she is three or four weeks in whelp do not suddenly find you will be on holiday!

Choosing the stud dog

There are three ways of choosing a stud dog. You can use a complete outcross in no way related to your bitch's pedigree. You can line-breed to a dog or bitch in both pedigrees, of known quality, dominant for reproducing good qualities and soundness of construction. Or you can in-breed, mating mother to son or father to daughter, which I do not advocate unless you are a very experienced breeder, undertaking the mating for a particular reason, with complete information on the background of all the dogs in the pedigrees. Outcross matings are rather hit and miss since you do not know the background of the other pedigree or whether it suits your particular breeding. Eventually, if

Below: *Mrs Valerie Birkin's Sansue kennel title holders (L to R):Sansue Phoebe, Sansue Royal Fancy, Sansue Wrainbow, Gaineda Consolidator of Sansue, Sansue Golden Ruler.*

line breeding, you reach the point where you have to outcross but very often you can make it a half outcross, keeping part of the stud dog's pedigree similar to your own. Personally I have found line-breeding very safe, producing soundness, quality and good temperament in the puppies. Do your homework, ask questions and find out what the background of your chosen stud dog produces, both faults and virtues.

The next thing to consider is where you want to improve on your bitch. You should choose a stud which will improve her faults and complement her virtues, and have a compatible pedigree. Some studs suit certain lines better than others. Take advice from experienced breeders, or better, from your own breeder if you have one. Take advice from a trusted breeder, not from one who will automatically have just the dog for your bitch! If

your hip score is not as good as you would like, choose a dog which is producing good hips. Not all dogs with a low score *produce* good scores. Ask to see scores and eye certificates and produce your own. Remember eye certificates should be up to date.

Go to the Championship or Specialty Shows to view the stud dogs on offer. See if anything in particular appeals, and if so, have a chat with his owner and ask for his pedigree. Use a known stud dog with a professional approach to his work. Do not use the Golden in the next road whose owner would like him to mate a bitch. You will not do him any favours, since without a

Below: *Mrs Anne Woodcock's Stanroph kennel title holders: Stanroph Spring Fantasy, Stanroph Soldier Boy, Stanroph Sailor Boy and Stanroph Steal a Glance.*

regular supply of bitches he will roam the neighbourhood in search and be a public menace. Probably, his owner will not want to go to the expense of X-rays and eye certificates.

Having made your choice, enquire the cost of the stud fee and state your wish to use him. When your bitch comes on heat and you see *continuous red* blood, telephone the stud dog owner and make a provisional date when you expect to mate her. This is very important since a good stud dog has a pretty full diary. Keep a daily check on your bitch and make sure she does not go out of season and then start again a few days later. This is very important as you would then have to start counting your days from the second time.

When to mate and pre-whelping care

Some bitches are mated on their 7th day, some as late as the 26th day, but these are exceptions to the more usual times. Generally speaking, the 11th to 14th days seem most likely. When the day draws near there are lots of signs to help you 'get it right'. The first thing you will notice is that the area around the vulva becomes very sensitive, and when grooming in that area the tail will fly round to the side or over her back. However, some bitches do this from day two, so you have to take other things into consideration. The vulva will become very swollen and the thick red blood will become thinner and very pale pink or almost creamy yellow. Also, just above the vulva beneath the anus you will see a wrinkled, shrivelled piece of skin rather like elephant hide. This will be very hard but when she is actually ready it will feel like a sponge. I find most novice owners find this easier to understand. Once these signs are apparent, ring your stud dog owner and fix the final day to visit your stud dog. Likewise, if the bitch is not ready for the provisional date you have made, let the stud dog owner know. Take her along on mating

day wearing a collar and lead and with all the relevant documents.

Your puppies will be due 63 days after mating and this is an easy period for you. Firstly, keep your eye on her until she dries up and do not let another dog get at her. She will need little extra attention until she is about seven weeks pregnant. You can take her to the veterinarian at about three and a half weeks to see if he or she thinks the bitch is in whelp. Sometimes they can tell and sometimes not, but by six weeks you should see a difference in her shape; when she has eaten and lies down like a lion you will see her sides very swollen. Early signs are pink teats, and where the breast bone descends sharply to the loin, underneath it will feel rather like a suet pudding. Again, false pregnancies produce the same signs.

After mating she should lead her normal daily life, her usual food and walks. At seven weeks, split her meals into two and by the 8th week you may have to go to three if she is very heavy. Double her meat ration at seven weeks but she will not have much room for many biscuits. Give her biggest meal in the morning as she will get very uncomfortable in the evening. Perhaps give a light fish meal in the evening, such as grilled herrings, which have a high nutritional value. I do not give any vitamins or additives before whelping but pump them in afterwards. This prevents enormous puppies causing difficult delivery. I once had a bitch who was very sick all through her pregnancy and subsequently died giving birth to nine puppies. Those puppies never knew their mother, never had colostrum protection nor much in the way of nutrition prior to birth. Three became champions and all nine were bonny with excellent bone, which proved you can pump it in after birth.

During those nine weeks you will prepare the quarters for the new family. If you have not got a kennel, select a place where she can be quiet and comfortable giving her family her undivided attention.

Prepare a 4ft by 4ft (1.2 x 1.2m) whelping box made from chip board with fairly high sides. (One sheet makes the floor and four sides.) The front opening should be half the height of the sides and be detachable. You will need a pig rail 2in (5cm) wide fixed about 3 to 4in (7.6-10cm) from the floor and about 3in (7.6cm) from the sides, which prevents the mother squashing her puppies. Paint the inside of the box with polyurethane varnish, since this makes it easy to wash. You will need at least two of the synthetic furry dog rugs that are machine washable, or whatever bedding you decide to use. Place newspaper underneath and all the mess from whelping or the puppies urine will soak through leaving the bed dry. You will need an infra-red lamp to hang over the box suspended by a chain, which can be adjusted up or down according to the temperature. Finally, for the whelping, a pile of clean towels; sharp scissors; a mild, non-toxic disinfectant; a lubricating gel or cooking oil; a thermometer and Iodine.

Whelping

If carrying a large litter bitches can whelp as much as seven days early and the pups are full-term size, but the poor mother could not carry them any longer. Likewise, if there are only one or two, a bitch could whelp seven days late. In this latter case you should have her checked by your veterinarian regularly who will feel her internally to find out when the cervix is opening and estimate how long she will take. He may suggest a Caesarian if things are looking bad, but no veterinarian these days rushes into this if it is possible to whelp normally.

When whelping day arrives, or rather the first stages, do not expect everything to go by the letter of the book. Each bitch is different — you learn every time. The first stages can be very trying for *you*, sometimes not long but they can go on for days and you begin to despair of anything happening. Usually they go off all

food about 24 hours before, but I once had a bitch go five days in this state before producing a litter normally! Some are still eating an hour before giving birth. Your bitch could dig holes to have her puppies for two weeks before whelping or perhaps only five hours. She will try to get behind the furniture or she may want to have them on your bed. Do not take any notice of her — find a hefty spring cleaning job or some freezer cooking to occupy you whilst keeping her near you and observe without fussing.

Once the second stage commences she may decide to shred paper in her box, but if not let her be and once she is either about to or has produced the first puppy she will allow you to persuade her that the box is best for her and her puppies. Do keep calm since any tension will upset her. A bitch's normal temperature is 101°F (38.3°C) and when about to whelp, this will start to descend to 99°F (37.2°C) or even as low as 97°F (36.1°C). This is a clear indication that things are really happening. She will also start to have a sticky white discharge and when the water starts pouring from her you know you are in business. Should you see a dark green discharge before any puppies arrive, seek veterinary help immediately. This usually signifies a dead puppy obstructing the whelping.

Rather than sitting up all night in a kennel, I have my own way of whelping. I cover my hall floor with a thick vinyl sheet in one of the alcoves. I then take very large, cardboard boxes and cut the sides to make one enormous box and pin the edges with pegs. In this goes the newspaper and rug, and I set up my quarters where I am shut off from the household, have the telephone and can make a hot drink. If I have to call the veterinarian night or day, he comes in the front door and none of the other dogs are disturbed. If I need an extra pair of hands, I am within screaming distance!

When everything is over, I leave

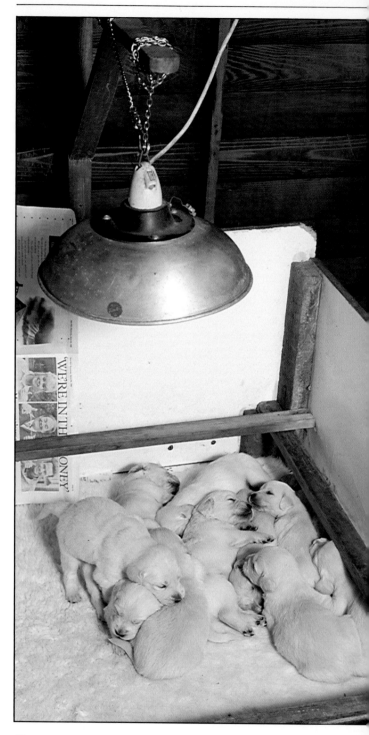

the bitch for a few hours to see how she handles the puppies, and then firmly put them in my basket and take her to her clean quarters, which have had the benefit of the infra-red lamp during whelping. If it gets cold, I have the advantage of the central heating. Once the bitch is comfortably settled in her clean box, all the debris can be burnt. If she whelps through the night, I put her out at breakfast time, but if in the morning, late afternoon. However, I am constantly peering through the kennel window to see that all is well. Some prefer to sleep with the litter for a few nights but I feel the bitch should be left quietly to cope.

You will barely see the first contractions but they will get very strong just before the first puppy appears. After that I find that the puppies just slip away with barely a big hiccup! The bitch seems almost unaware of the puppies' arrival and I have to feel under the tail and start work. The textbooks tell you that the sac of membranes appears first, but in all my years of whelping I have only experienced this once!

If your bitch is having her first litter or is very full of puppies, it is as well to give her a hand. With the first few puppies she will not be able to get round to her rear end. If you leave her to it, you may well lose valuable puppies which will upset her greatly. Keep a record of each puppy, sex, time of birth, with or without afterbirth. This will be helpful if you have to call the veterinarian. Have towels at hand, loads of clean newspaper, scissors standing in diluted, non-toxic disinfectant and a plastic sack for rubbish. Wait for your first puppy, towel in hand. It may arrive in a rush or more likely it will be firmly jammed by a big head before the vulva has stretched, in which case oil the edge of the vulva and gently stretch it. Never pull the puppy but

try to ease it through gently. Once past the shoulders it will tumble out. If the afterbirth is attached and still inside the bitch, wait for it to arrive or when you can get it safely without tearing. In the meanwhile, break the tough sac and release the liquid. When you have the afterbirth, take the puppy in a towel and cut the cord about 4in (10cm) from the abdomen. With new mums, or even bitches who like to do their own work, I am always cautious with cords since they can be too rough, causing hernias. Sometimes haemorrhaging is caused by the bitch biting the cord too close to the abdomen. In the latter case, apply an iodine pressure pad to the spot.

Support the puppy's head underneath the chin and the back of the head with your thumb and fingers and rub roughly with a towel, holding the puppy's head towards the floor and making strong downward movements to extract any fluid from the nostrils and lungs. Shake and rub vigorously — puppies are not fragile provided the head and neck are supported firmly. Watch how the bitch knocks them roughly around the box to get them going. It is vital to get rid of all the fluid, and if you hear it rattling in the lungs try again. Gently put the puppy to the teat and let the bitch lick him, open his mouth gently with thumb and finger and get the teat inside at the same time as expressing a little milk. If the puppy does not immediately suckle, stroke his back in an upward movement and this usually works.

Events usually proceed more easily after the first born, and puppies suckling certainly induce the arrival of the family. You may find two or three arriving as on a conveyor belt! You have to move fast or have help at hand. I once delivered nine puppies in one and a half hours, leaving both the bitch and myself nervous wrecks! An even-interval delivery is the ideal. If, at any time, proceedings slow up — an interval of perhaps two hours with weak contractions — then

Left: *Tiny puppies sleeping comfortably under the warmth of an infra-red lamp. Note the pig rail inside the box.*

consult your veterinarian. A dead puppy may be holding up progress, or the bitch may need a stimulant to deliver the remainder of the litter.

The most petrifying experience is to be faced with two tiny feet and a tail protruding with no membranous sac. Here, you must move fast since the puppy may drown in the fluid or suffocate in the pelvis. Quite often at this point, the bitch decides to have a rest and you have to induce pushing and a sense of urgency from her. For some unknown reason, I push my hand very hard down her back to the tail, oil the vulva, and scream at her to push! Whether this is the right method, I do not know, but in my experience the puppy usually arrives with a big plop when you have almost given up! The worst

presentation you can possibly have is a sideways diagonal. This is a puppy lying on its side presenting its shoulder to the pelvis cornerwise. This usually needs the professional help of a veterinarian. I have only experienced it twice and the first time the vet gave a deft twist and the puppy arrived safely, but he assured me I could not have done it. The second time the puppy had to be repeatedly pushed back inside the bitch and attempts were made to turn it to the correct position. Just as we were about to depart for a Caesarian, it arrived alive!

During the whelping have a bowl of glucose water at hand for the bitch's refreshment. Do not give milk or any other food. If she should require a caesarian, she

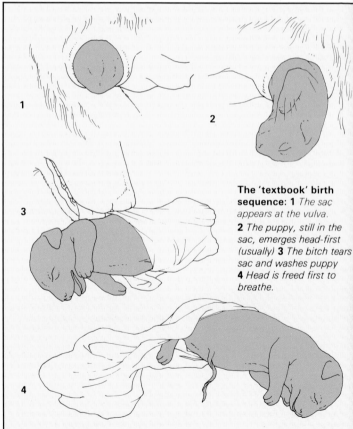

The 'textbook' birth sequence: 1 *The sac appears at the vulva.*
2 *The puppy, still in the sac, emerges head-first (usually)* **3** *The bitch tears sac and washes puppy* **4** *Head is freed first to breathe.*

needs to be empty for the anaesthetic. When you have a fair number of puppies in the nest, put the bitch on a lead and take her out to relieve herself. Before letting her back in the box, run your hands down her ribs and loin and try to estimate how many more bumps you can feel. When you feel she is finally finished, call the veterinarian and arrange a visit from him or her to confirm this and to administer a pituitrin shot to clear the womb, close the uterus and prevent any infection. If the bitch finishes in the early hours, I usually telephone before surgery for a visit, but otherwise I expect the veterinarian to make a visit during the day. If you have abnormal problems, do not hesitate to call the veterinarian day or night. My own vet always says 'do not hestiate — a puppy's life may be at stake'. Be sure you have a veterinarian who will visit and not expect you to take the bitch to surgery, which will unsettle her and run the risk of infection.

If your bitch should be unlucky enough to undergo a Caesarian, there are a few tips I can give you. Put the puppies either in a box or on the rug under a very low-slung, infra-red lamp and go to the veterinarian with the bitch. When she returns she will still be under sedation and feel a little unwell. She will be rather bewildered about what these bundles are and where they have come from. Give the puppies a good feed from her when she returns, then leave her to sleep it off in her box under the lamp. Either put the puppies in another box under another lamp or put them in a box on a heated trolley. They will be quite content with a full tummy and the warmth. When she is fully recovered, take her family to her and let them feed. Sit with her to ensure she is ready for them and coping, and when all is well leave her to enjoy her family in peace.

Once whelping is finally completed, give the bitch a light meal and my best recipe for nutrition: milk and Gyrima Gruel to restore the nervous system. Take a cup of porridge oats, two cups of water, an egg, a big spoonful of honey, another of a powder used to make a restorative milk drink and another of Glucose and boil up your porridge until thick. Then dilute it with a cup of milk and cool. Bitches love it and it will form a major part of their diet in the next week to ten days.

Finally, make sure she relieves herself and settle her comfortably in her new quarters with her puppies. I personally always leave the electric light on all night so that she can see what she is doing. It is probably totally unnecessary but it makes me happy, especially with a new mother.

Eclampsia
After whelping, if your bitch behaves restlessly, hysterically, runs a temperature or vomits, seek veterinary assistance *immediately*. It could be the onset of eclampsia, caused by calcium deficiency. The vet will give an intravenous calcium injection. It can also, rarely, occur during whelping.

Rearing your litter
There is insufficient space in these pages to go deeply into this subject, so I will go through the essentials. More explicit, day-to-day instructions can be found in *Rearing and Selling a Litter*, written by myself and obtainable from The Secretary of the Golden Retriever Club (UK — see Appendix) sold in the aid of rescue funds.

The first essential is to keep a close eye on your bitch and the puppies, sitting with her and observing. Is each puppy feeding; is each puppy being washed; is your bitch content; is she hysterical, distressed or fussing? If there are any signs of problems, seek veterinary advice. It is in the first ten days when things can go wrong and constant attention will pick up signs immediately, and you will therefore stand more chance of success in solving problems. In the first two to three weeks you will have little to do but keep your bitch well fed. For the first 24 hours I feed Gyrima Gruel three times but only once with an egg. If everything is digested well, I then give a light fish meal and two Gruels; at the end of the second day, her first meat meal. She should now have three meat meals and two Gruels daily. She may not take the maximum quantities until the puppies make more demands on her and she will probably refuse gruel after ten days. I estimate to feed 1lb (453g) meat for every two puppies she is feeding and break this down into three or four meals

daily. Fresh water should be available at all times in her quarters and she should have peace and quiet to enjoy her family.

Make sure the milk is flowing freely and that each puppy is getting its fair share. If you have a large litter of ten or more, you will find that half suckle and the others sleep and then they change the shifts! If they do not look nicely rounded, you may have to top them up with a powdered puppy milk or evaporated milk diluted as instructed on the tin. With a small

litter, you will have to ensure that none of the teats become hard with mastitis. If this should occur, warm cloths will soften and ease the situation and the milk must be expressed.

Keep puppies at a comfortable temperature. If they are too hot they will sprawl round the edges of the box, in which case raise the height of the lamp or turn off altogether. If they are cold, they will huddle in a heap, in which case lower the lamp. Ideally they should feel warm to the touch.

Just in case you have time on your hands, remember to check the puppies' nails regularly and clip at least once a week while feeding from mum. Otherwise they will tear her tummy and could be a good reason for her to avoid going into the box. You should also check to see if their ears are clean. The whelping box and kennel should be cleaned with disinfectant each day. Mother should not be taken out for walks in case she should bring any infection back to her babies.

Before weaning, *worming:* I would wean a large litter at two to two and a half weeks and an average litter at three weeks. Therefore, worming would take place the day before weaning. If puppies have bright yellow, curdy motions at approximately two weeks, I worm immediately but always by three weeks using a liquid preparation, measuring the correct dosage for weight and administering with a small plastic syringe obtainable from your veterinarian. I carry on worming every seven days until I see no more worms. You probably will not see anything on the first worming since you are really just releasing some of the eggs. If you do not see worms at all, you have not given the right dose! Your bitch should also be wormed a few days later since she has had the awful task of cleaning the puppies.

Puppies of two to three weeks will not be very steady on their feet, nor are they able to lap very quickly. So my puppies have a knob of chopped raw beef mince for their first meal. They sit on my knee and feed from my hand, and how they quiver with excitement when they smell it. It is easy to squeeze pieces into their mouths and they soon learn to tear away at it. I try to ensure that mum has been absent for a couple of hours so they are hungry, and when she

Left: *Three week-old puppies beginning to be aware of sounds, surroundings and taking their first steps.*

returns they do not tear at her teats so roughly. If the meat is well digested, the next day I try two meat meals. I like to feed meat individually and at first it is sufficient to put piles of meat around the box, but later I use small shallow bowls and divide the slow feeders from the fast feeders. This keeps you active if you have a large litter! Now they are having 1oz (28g) meat in the morning and 1oz (28g) in the evening. Each week this should be increased by 1oz (28g) on one of the meals but not on both. As the puppies' rations increase, so mum's rations reduce until they are fully weaned at about five weeks and the bitch will return to her normal diet. I do not introduce biscuit to puppies until about five weeks since I find that if anything upsets their stomachs it is the puppy meal, although the new small formulations for puppies and toy dogs does not have this effect and they love it.

After seven days, I introduce them to milk using a good quality powdered milk for puppies, or evaporated milk diluted as instructed or goat's milk, mixed with either a baby cereal or wheat cereal rusks. I use shallow baking trays so they do not have far to lap, and they all feed together in two or three trays. Keep dipping their heads in it until they know what to do. They will fall in it and get it all over the place, but after a couple of days they will be cleaner. I allow a pint of milk (20fl oz/0.6l) daily for each puppy but they will not take their full quantity until about six weeks. I always give a meat meal at the beginning of the day and just before bedtime since I believe they must be very hungry in the morning and the evening meal sustains them through the night. With small litters of two to four puppies, if mum has plenty of milk I do not introduce lapping until perhaps five weeks.

At about four weeks, I entice mum back into the house at night and my bitches will willingly exchange a kennel for warmth and companionship beside the bed, where they cannot hear puppy

noises. By five to six weeks, the bitch is merely draining her milk off morning and evening and is very glad to leave her family in your capable hands. Once weaning commences I have my bitches indoors for their family evening.

At about four weeks, I take the front completely away from the box to introduce the puppies to cleanliness and geography. Soon they will also be interested in exploring the world beyond their kennel.

Daily meal schedule

9 am	Meat meal
12 noon	Milk drink
3 pm	Milk with cereal
6 pm	Milk with cereal
10 pm	Meat meal

(If more convenient reverse order of last two meals).

Prevention of disease
There is a very high risk of infection in the form of Parvo-virus being brought into the kennel from visitors. Yet the more people puppies meet, the better they are socialized. Some people keep a tray of disinfectant at their gate, either bleach or the Parvo-wash, and insist visitors dip their shoes in it, since they are the most likely source of infection. Another excellent idea is to keep a plastic spray of Parvo-wash at the gate to spray shoes. Always insist on fresh clothes when people visit the puppies and on no account let anyone visit straight from a show.

The puppies will be ready for their new homes at seven to eight weeks and you have now gone full cycle, presenting your owners with a full diet sheet, pedigree and registration certificate, together with instructioins on worming and vaccinations.

Placing your puppies
Puppies do not ask to be born and it is essential that you are absolutely certain that you have the correct home for each individual. Although time-consuming, I like to meet

buyers at one week, four and seven weeks, which gives potential owners plenty of time to assess and discover the type of puppy they need. If people took more trouble at this stage, we would not be re-homing so many 'rescue' dogs. A quiet, shy or timid puppy will be unsuitable for a young, rumbustious family. Nor should a boisterous puppy go to a quiet, elderly couple. If you have any doubts, do some detective work on your buyer and if you have any doubts at all, simply do not sell. Buyers who have just lost their elderly Golden are usually okay, but even they may have forgotten what a handful puppies can be and they may be 14 years older themselves! Encourage the children to see the puppies and watch their behaviour towards them and the control the parents have over their children. Finally, ask all the questions *you* were asked when purchasing your puppy. Make sure your buyers understand that if they have to part with their puppy, for any personal or economic reason — for any reason at all, not just if something goes wrong with their puppy — they should come back to you because you care and would like the opportunity of re-homing it suitably.

A stud dog's career

Think very carefully if you are considering using your dog at public stud. Once he has been used and knows the facts of life, he will need a regular supply of bitches to satisfy his natural instincts. The pet dog will not have this opportunity and he may well go in search.

It is usually the top show-winning dogs of good pedigree that are in demand at stud, with good hip scores and up-to-date eye certificates. He should be of such quality and merit, in temperament and conformation, to be considered as being able to maintain or improve the breed.

Should you decide you have such an exceptional dog, he should not be used too early in life. Usually males are proved around ten to twelve months, but much depends on a suitable bitch appearing on the scene. He should be well grown before the event, since some people hold the view that males do not grow on any more after a proving stud. Similarly, some people take the view that bitches do not continue to grow after their first season. The ideal first bitch is one who has had litters and is a real tart to show him what to do. Whilst not inhibiting his first efforts, do make sure from the start that he gets used to the idea of being handled and realizes that he may well need your assistance in guiding him. He may well have difficult bitches where he cannot manage on his own. He will soon turn to you and say 'Oh mum, what can I do?' and rely on your help and advice! Do not give him too many bitches in his first year at stud, if he should be so lucky! He will be too excited and think he is every bitch's dream, making him a thorough nuisance at shows.

The bitch should visit the dog and you should establish where the best place is for matings to take place, then stick to it. With a young dog, do not take him off his home territory where he is confident. Sometimes, in later life, it may be necessary but not in the learning stage. Bring him out to the chosen place on a lead and let him have a flirt and a chance to 'chat up' the bitch for a minute or two or as long as it takes to get her in a receptive mood. Then get the deed done as quickly as possible before she changes her mind!

When you own a stud dog, you develop a very close understanding of one another and establish a lifetime's rapport. He will quickly realize when bitches are ready or not. Have faith in his knowledge of scent. You will soon realize when he is doing the stud to please you or because she is very exciting. While you are learning together, he will develop a fixation with you, because are you not the one from whom all blessings flow? Food, walks, bitches — all the good things in his life!

Hall of Fame

Ch Styal Scott of Glengilde

Ch Nortonwood Faunus

Ch Camrose Cabus Christopher

Ch Gaineda Consolidator of Sansue

Christopher won 41 Challenge Certificates, produced 26 title holders and held the Alison Nairn Stud Dog Progeny Cup for six years. Christopher's grandson, Scott, holds the present day breed record in England with 42 CCs.

Scott's sire, Faunus (a Christopher son) held the cup for seven years and produced 17 title holders. An excellent example of line breeding producing successful results. Consolidator is the current holder of the same cup.

Ch Styal Susila – puppy

Ch Styal Stephanie of Camrose

Rossbourne Quality Miss

Sh Ch Stanroph Spring Fantasy

Stephanie and Susila are litter sisters and Christopher daughters. Stephanie is the breed record holder in England with 27 Challenge Certificates. Susila is the holder of 10 CCs and dam of four title holders. Rossbourne Quality Miss, owned and bred by Mr and Mrs R Burnett, was Best Bitch at Crufts 1997. Stanroph Spring Fantasy, owned and bred by Mrs A Woodcock, is the youngest bitch champion in the breed at two years old.

Chapter Seven

SHOWS AND SHOWING

THE Kennel Club makes the rules and regulations under which all shows are run in the UK. You should obtain a copy of these from the Kennel Club and familiarize yourself with what is expected of you and your dog.

Your dog will have been registered at The Kennel Club by the breeder but, in order to show, it must then be transferred into your ownership, since the dog must be the registered property of the person entering the show.

You should take your puppy to

Below: *A quality puppy with show potential; a good example of the breed standard. Careful rearing and exercise will help the puppy fulfil its potential.*

ringcraft classes as soon as he has completed his vaccination programme. The Breed Clubs usually run regular classes for Goldens where you will get first-class instruction and soon both of you will know what is expected. There are also mixed breed ringcraft classes in most areas. You should also visit two or three shows, without your puppy, to take in the quality you will be competing against. This will also be instructive if you watch the handling closely, particularly by the top breeders.

Take your puppy back to his breeder and seek his or her advice on whether he is good enough to show. Even if he was selected as a show puppy, you can only say he was show potential at eight weeks and now is the time to assess whether he is fulfilling expectations. Golden entries are usually the largest in any show and competition is very high. Shows are advertised in the weekly dog papers *(Dog World* or *Our Dogs* in the UK) and will give the name of the Secretary to contact for a

Schedule. When this arrives read it carefully, including the small print, and then complete the entry form and, together with entry fees, send it off before the closing date.

Your dog should be in good condition, the right weight and in good coat. Watch his diet strictly, reducing or increasing when necessary, particularly watching the carbohydrates. Never show him when out of coat. In Goldens the classes are huge and coatless dogs do not stand much chance. Also you will not want people to see your dog looking poor.

Which shows should you enter? Again, seek advice from your breeder who will know which judges like her stock, or from an experienced exhibitor. Our breed standard specifies that Goldens may be any shade of gold or cream, but not red or mahogany. Some

Below: *A well-trained Golden moving correctly toward the judge having done his homework and learnt his lessons well.*

judges are advocates of one extreme or the other. In appreciating cream they usually decry the very dark, and vice versa. This is bad judging policy, but if you have either extreme end of the colour chart it is wise to seek advice, since there is no point in wasting money and time travelling if you have a cream and the judge likes darkest gold! The same applies in reverse.

Types of show in England

There are Exemption Shows, which are really the fun events and do not require a dog to be Kennel Club registered. There are Sanction Shows which are restricted to members of the promoting society, excluding dogs in classes higher than post-graduate or who have Challenge Certificates. Limited Shows are confined to members of the Society and exclude Challenge Certificate winners. Then we come to the Open Shows where breed classes are scheduled as well as Variety classes and you would be well advised to try your luck in the breed class at a local Open Show for your first venture. Try a few of these to gain confidence and see how you do. The Championship Shows are the really important events and only they have Challenge Certificates on offer — which is the ultimate aim! Goldens are scheduled at all the General Championship Shows, the Gundog Group Shows and the Breed Clubs' Championship Shows, so the show calendar is pretty full!

English judging system

This is straightforward. The judge examines each dog and asks the handler to run with the dog, usually in a triangle. He or she then looks at all dogs in the class collectively before finally selecting his or her best five and places them in order of merit from one to five. At an Open Show, all unbeaten dogs come back into the ring and the judge chooses the Best of Breed. At a Championship Show, all unbeaten dogs challenge for the Challenge Certificate (three of

which under three different judges make a show Champion). If the dog has already won a Show Gundog Qualifying Certificate or at least a Certificate of Merit at a Field Trial, then he would become a full Champion. Finally the Dog CC and the Bitch CC winners challenge one another for Best of Breed who will be the selected representative of the breed to compete in the Gundog Group.

Right: *Final line-up of the Open Dog Class at Richmond Championship Show, England — all immaculately presented.*

Below: *Having moved for the judge, this Golden stands freely in show position for the judge's final inspection.*

Shows in the USA

There are American Kennel Club Sanctioned Matches given by Specialty and All-breed Clubs for pure-bred dogs competing on an informal basis. No Championship points are awarded. These events provide an excellent opportunity for exhibitors to gain show experience.

The main type of show is either a Specialty Show for one breed or the All-breed Regional Show at top level, which offers Puppy, Novice, Bred by Exhibitor, American-bred and Open Classes for each sex. Champions have a separate class, and the dogs earn points towards their titles through wins from the classes, in competition for best of winners and placings in the ultimate groups. There are seven groups in all and the Golden Retriever is shown in the Sporting Group.

Below: *Yet another wet summer show in England! Exhibitors at Windsor making best use of wet weather accommodation.*

Scandinavian and Continental methods of judging

The judging system is quite different in these countries and this also presents difficulties when we have judges from abroad judging in England. They are unfamiliar with our system, find it alien and are not prepared for the large entries.

In Scandinavia and the rest of Europe, there are Championship Shows, Breed Retriever/Spaniel Championship Shows and International Championship Shows. Only International Championship Shows award a CACIB (Certificat d'Aptitude au Championat International de Beauté), the others only a CAC (Certificat d'Aptitude au Championat). There are few classes. Sometimes, nowadays, there are baby puppy classes for three to six-month old dogs, but I do not care for them. The young class is 9 to 18 months. Anything over that age is in the Open Class. Champions are confined to Champions Class. They cannot compete for CAC but can compete

Above: *In contrast, sunshine over the show rings at the Richmond show — an enormously popular event.*

for CACIB which would make them International Champions. CAC brings the title of Champion if gaining three CACs, under different judges. Breed Championships usually also schedule Veteran and Field Trial Classes.

The judge examines each dog and first grades them, and subsequently they are judged for competition. Each dog has to be given a critique in triplicate — one copy is given to the exhibitor, one copy goes to the Breeds Breeding Committee and one to the Kennel Club. As this is a fairly lengthy process one is allocated not only a steward but a ring secretary who valiently writes to dictation from the judge — in English if the judge is from England. Each exhibit is examined, moved, the critique dictated and a grade given: 1st = excellent; 2nd = some faults but still good; 3rd = far more important faults — fair; zero = either bad tempered or would not allow the judge to get his or her hands on him! Fortunately the latter are few. Having examined all the exhibits in the class, only the firsts may re-enter for the competitive judging. Here, we return to the English type of judging by the judge placing the first five or six in order of merit, one to six. Any of these final winners can be given a certificate of quality and/or a prize of honour.

Having judged the Young and Open Classes, all the First prize winners and the top five from the Young Class return to the ring and just five will be placed. The final winner from these five will receive the CAC, who will then compete with the winner of champions for the CACIB, if this is on offer. If judging both dogs and bitches, the winners return to the ring to be placed number one in show, two, three, four and five regardless of sex.

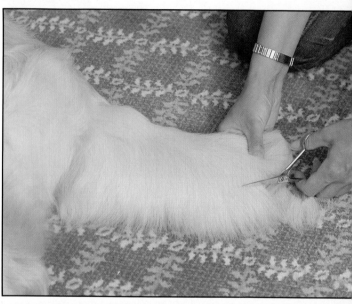

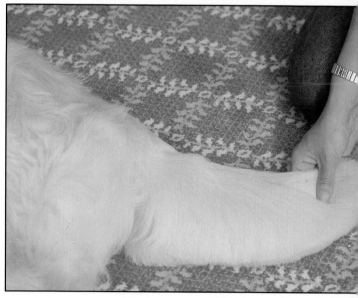

Show grooming

Your Golden must be trimmed to full advantage. You will be well advised to attend a trimming demonstration by your nearest Breed Club, but if this is not possible ask your breeder or an experienced exhibitor, who presents their Goldens perfectly, for advice and instruction.

Basically you are trimming him to show off his good points. Goldens do not need a vast amount of trimming and it should commence about two weeks before the show. The tail is trimmed with ordinary straight scissors. Feel with your left hand the end bone in the tail and

Left: *The procedure for correctly trimming a very thick Golden tail: start beyond the end bone and trim in a fan shape.*

Below left: *The final result should look like this: neat and tidy, giving balance and outline to your Golden's body.*

Below: *Tackling thick, long hair on neck and shirtfront. The thinning scissors are used underneath the long top hair.*

trim leaving about ½in (1.3cm) beyond your left hand and continue upwards in a fan shape leaving about 4in (10cm) of feathering at the longest part.

His shirt front, neck and shoulders should be tackled very carefully. It is better to make two or three attempts than to take out too much at once. Goldens are attractive with their long hair and feathering and I do hate the practice sometimes currently used of shaving the hair almost down to the roots on the shirt front. Thinning scissors, with very fine blades, should be used and the scissor marks should not be visible. Use upward movements and constantly comb the hair until the shirt front looks tidy and in a good shape.

Careful attention to trimming the neck and shoulders should then be tackled with the thinning scissors. Always cut the way the hair grows and use the scissors underneath the top layer of hair, which will then lay flat enhancing the outline and hiding the scissors marks. Trim the hair beneath the ear very short, between the shirt front and neck until it is tidy. The long hair on top and around the ear flap should

be taken out so that the ear is neatly shaped. A razor comb can be used here, or pluck out a few hairs at a time between thumb and finger in the direction of hair growth.

Tidy up any trouser feathering which is hiding the hock angulation and take off excess hair from foot to hock. I use the thinning scissors for this area. Comb the hair up towards the hock from the foot and then keep cutting with the thinning scissors, comb flat and continue until the hair flattens. Finally, trim round the shape of the feet with straight scissors. Take away the excess hair between the toes and centre of the pad to the top of the foot and carefully trim with thinning scissors until you achieve a good outline. Shape the foot by trimming lengthy hair around the top of the foot.

Bathing

Bath as near to the show date as possible with one or two exceptions. Owners of straight-coated dogs have an easier life, since there is little to do after

bathing. Wavy-coated dogs have to be bathed earlier since it takes a lot of work to get them dry with the waves in place and no tufts of hair sticking up. If you have a dog with an extremely thick coat, he will have to be bathed a couple of days before the show to allow time for the coat to settle.

Although it is possible to use human shampoo to bathe your dog, it is preferable to use a special dog shampoo. These preparations are formulated to care for the coat without causing irritation to the skin.

From time to time you may also choose to use an insecticidal shampoo. In this instance, the manufacturer's instructions should be followed carefully. Always ensure that you have rinsed your dog thoroughly after any bath so that no shampoo residue is left behind which could aggravate the skin.

Below: *Thinning the thick hair behind and below the ears with thinning scissors. Trim in the direction of hair growth.*

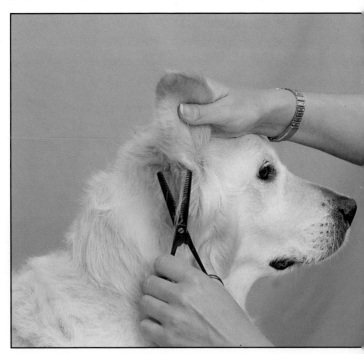

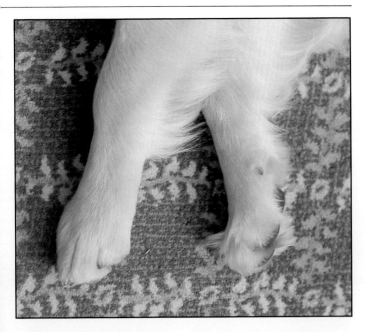

Above: *The right foot has not yet been trimmed; the left foot beautifully presented — but well-shaped feet help!*

Below: *If wondering whether or not to bath your Golden, always do it. Here, a show bitch is being bathed for a big show.*

The drying process is very important. If a dog is straight-coated, towel him briskly, comb the hair into place and leave it to dry naturally. If your Golden has a more difficult or wavy coat, you will have to put him in a warm place and continually comb the coat until dry. If you cannot spare the time, wrap him up in a large towel to soak up the damp and then comb the coat into place. If you can get your Golden accustomed to a hairdryer and give the coat a blow-dry, you will produce a more professional result. Blow-drying lifts the hair and separates every strand giving a lovely sheen.

Naturally, your Golden must be bathed if dirty, but most dogs benefit from a bath before each major show. Presentation is so important in large classes and you must do all you can to give your Golden as much chance as possible.

Show bag
The day before the show you will have to prepare your show bag. It should contain a blanket or bench blanket, if the show is benched (in

Above: *A well-adjusted Golden benched comfortably at Windsor '88, illustrating the breed's calm, confident temperament.*

the UK, not many Open Shows are benched but all Championship Shows are); a towel in case your dog gets wet; a water bowl and water container; his favourite titbits for 'ring bait'; your hound glove and comb; some spirit cleaner in case your Golden gets dirty; a benching chain and collar (if a benched show); a show lead of the ribbon, slip-lead type so that you can roll it back over his shoulders to display his neck; a ring clip for your number (UK); exhibitor's pass and car park sticker.

Show day

Allow plenty of time to get to the show. Do not rush in at the last minute in a panic. Exercise your dog on arrival and bench him comfortably. You have already trimmed and prepared your dog and all that remains to do on show day is a quick brush and comb.

There are two ways of showing your Golden — free standing or stacking. Basically you are trying to display his good points to advantage and the method you use should be the one which does this best. If you have several dogs, it does not mean that the same method suits them all, so you must adjust yourself to both. It is wise to use titbits to ring bait and, if free standing, walk your dog into position and stand in front with a titbit, taking care he does not sink his head into his shoulders when looking up at you. Talk to him all the time and perhaps he will also wag his tail. If you have a restless dog or you want to emphasize a good neck, tail set or outline, it may be preferable to set him up. Move his legs into the correct position, hold out his tail level with his back and hold a titbit under his nose, so that he will stretch his neck out to reach it. Practise at home for the most effective method, either in front of a long mirror or patio doors.

When you have shown your dog, do not go home immediately! Watch the experienced handlers and see what tips you can pick up. Watch the dogs and how the handlers correct any naughtiness or friskiness. Watch and learn to recognize good points and bad — and above all learn to recognize quality in Goldens.

Left: *One of two methods of showing the Golden to advantage — free standing, fore square and attentive to handler.*

Below: *The same Golden, displaying an equally high ability in the second method of showing, ie stacking.*

Chapter Eight

WORKING GOLDEN RETRIEVERS

Gundog training

The Golden Retriever's natural attributes make him an ideal gundog, able to hunt and retrieve tenderly through the thickest cover. His dense, water-resistant coat provides excellent protection.

An eight week-old puppy is very receptive and eager to learn. He will seek out and carry all manner of articles, and this natural activity should never be discouraged, no

matter how unwanted the 'gift' may be. Gradually and with great patience, these basic instincts can be channelled so that the dog can eventually perform the many and varied tasks required of a gundog.

Although every correctly bred Golden will be capable of work, they will vary considerably in ability and certain breeding lines are better suited to this purpose.

Early training can be done at home taking the form of basic obedience (see Chapter Three). Use your dog's name together with the required discipline, eg 'Ben come, sit, wait, heel', etc. It is important to have your dog's attention and respect; he must respond immediately to your commands.

Do not make the all too familiar mistake of thinking your gundog requires at least ten retrieves daily. The retrieve is the final stage of your dog's basic training and should be restricted. If your dog does not come as soon as he is called, it is pointless thinking — or hoping! — he is going to bring a thrown dummy to hand. Until he is able to walk to heel calmly at your side on a loose lead, he will not be able to do so off the lead.

There are many specialist books written on the subject of gundog training (see Appendix). Local gundog societies hold training classes where you can learn how to teach your dog basic obedience, the appropriate whistle and verbal commands, directional training and retrieving from land and water. All these activities will be carried out on strange territory with the added distraction of other dogs and handlers. Eventually your dog will be introduced to gunfire, and it is essential that this is carried out under the supervision of an experienced trainer.

Left: *A successful retrieve from cover. Often scenting conditions are difficult and the dog must be tireless.*

Below: *Three Golden Retrievers at play in the water. The adults soon teach the youngsters to have confidence.*

Left: *This illustrates a lesson in attention. It is most important for the dog and handler to maintain good contact at all times.*

Below left: *The dog is being taught to walk to heel off the lead. The handler gives encouragement with both her voice and her hand.*

Bottom left: *'Get back' — a lesson in directional training, clearly instructed. As the dog gains confidence, the distances are increased.*

For gundog training, you will need some canvas covered dummies weighing approximately 1lb (453g). Use a lighter weight dummy for young dogs and puppies. An old sock stuffed with soft material is ideal for a puppy, and a plastic detergent container, again covered with an old sock, is suitable for the young dog and also makes an excellent dummy for use in the water. You will also need a bag for carrying the dummies, a whistle, a leather to dry the dog's coat after work, a slip lead, a check chain and a leather lead. As the name implies, the 'check' chain is for checking the dog during training and should *never* be worn otherwise. When the dog is out working, it is all too easy for any form of collar to be caught up in heavy cover, when jumping or swimming — often with heart-breaking results.

Many show exhibitors are becoming increasingly aware of the dual aspect of the Golden Retriever, gaining immense pleasure from working with their dogs.

Above all, training should be fun. Goldens respond best to firmness and kindness. Always give plenty of praise and reassurance, particularly to the young and apprehensive dog. Remember that your hands are for kindness and attention, *never* for chastisement.

Below: *Equipment required for basic training. Items are available from your local gundog club or gunsmiths.*

Working tests

In the UK, gundog societies hold competitive working tests which are classified as puppy, novice, intermediate and open.

Canvas dummies weighing approximately 1lb (453g) are used for retrieving. The usual procedure is for two judges to assess the dogs and handlers on a points system over at least four exercises. The exercises are suited to the required standard of the test and applicable to the work required of a Retriever on a shooting day.

Working tests are becoming increasingly popular. Most members of the family can participate and also enjoy a day out in the countryside. If you are not actually competing, you can assist, for example by throwing dummies, stewarding for the judges and competitors or preparing refreshments.

Those who do not have the opportunity or desire to take part at a shoot can still have the pleasure of working with their dog. Working tests are an excellent means of testing your dog's ability and training progress but can in no way simulate all the excitement and atmosphere of a real shooting day.

Picking-up

Once your dog has proven its ability at working tests, you may have the opportunity to 'pick-up' freshly shot game (ie pheasant, partridge, duck etc) during the shooting season. In this way, you can test your dog's ability on the 'real thing'. He must be steady at all times, never chasing live game and only leaving your side when directed to do so. The dog learns to hunt and follow the scent of injured game, retrieving in all types of cover as well as in and across water.

To collect wounded game as quickly as possible and retrieve tenderly to hand are the prime functions of a Retriever. It is important to carefully introduce your dog to game during his first shooting season and the number of retrievers should be restricted.

When training a new dog, an older, more experienced dog should always accompany you.

A well-trained dog is a great asset to a shoot and always welcome. Out in all weathers in beautiful countryside, a day's picking-up is exhausting but very rewarding.

UK field trials

In the UK, field trials are competitions held under Kennel Club rules during the shooting season on freshly shot game. The terrain is varied and often a great amount of walking across seemingly endless fields of stubble and sugarbeet is involved, testing the fitness of both dog and handler. This is termed a 'walk-up' trial. Dogs must be experienced in picking up all types of game and under good control so that they do not disturb unshot game out of the area in which they should be working.

Either three or four judges officiate at trials and grade the dogs by assessing the degree of difficulty of the retrieve and the quality of the dog's performance. The dogs are called into line in numerical order and judged in pairs. If a dog fails to find the shot bird, then another dog is given the opportunity to retrieve it, thus placing the successful dog in a strong position (this is termed an 'eye-wipe'). Dogs receiving a satisfactory grading under the first

Top right: *An early lesson in steadiness. Dummies are thrown around the dogs, tempting them to move. The handler praises and reassures the puppy.*

Above right: *The dog is being taught the commands to 'hold' and 'give'. The dummy is placed gently in the mouth and given to hand when requested.*

Right: *Training should finish with success and on a 'happy note'. If things have gone wrong, do a simple marked retrieve followed by praise.*

judge have the chance to try again under the next judge. Then all the successful dogs return to be scrutinized by all the judges and are placed accordingly.

Dogs must gain a qualification at a novice trial before they are eligible to enter a trial which carries a qualification towards the title of Field Trial Champion. In the UK, nominations to run in trials greatly exceed the number of available places – usually 12 dogs at a one-day trial and 24 dogs at a two-day qualifying trial.

was only crippled, another chance was given.

Excellence in Obedience is tested on a blind retrieve. The dogs are sent in a direction, expected to run in a line until reaching the 'fall'. Handlers use whistles to stop the dog when off course and hand signals bring them back on the right track.

Field trials today are divided into four groups: the Pointing dogs, the Scenting or Trailing Hounds, Retrievers (using both land and water) and Flushing dogs. Only

A summary of UK field trial rules

Eliminating faults: Hard mouth; whining or barking; running in and chasing; out of control; failure to enter water

Major faults: Failing to find game; unsteadiness at heel; 'eye-wipe'; disturbing ground; slack and unbusiness-like work; noisy handling; poor control; changing birds

Credit points: Natural ability in finding game; marking ability; good nose; drive; style; quickness in gathering game; control; quietness in handling; retrieving and delivery back to the handler

---

US field trials

The Golden Retriever Club of America gave their first trial in 1937. The outstanding temperament and ability portrayed in hunting gave a new insight to the Golden Retriever by dog people and hunters alike.

Because of the new popularity enjoyed by the three Retrievers, the field trials would have to change to accommodate the vast numbers of interested sportsmen. AKC trials were now 'open to all'. Briefly, tracking wounded game was eliminated. Each dog was given exactly the same test. The individual dogs were run from a line and must bring game back to the area. If a bird flew out of an area or

dogs entered in AKC licensed events may attain the coveted Dual Championship title. These dogs have completed all requirements in both conformation and field trial competitions.

There are many Golden Retriever clubs in the US offering field trial events and, more recenty, hunting tests under AKC rules. Due to the increasing interest in this sport there are frequent and necessary changes in the rules. To obtain information on updated AKC Regulations for Hunting Tests for Golden Retrievers and Field Trial Rules, contact the American Kennel Club (see Appendix for address). For information on area clubs and field trials write to the Secretary of the Golden Retriever Club of America, Ms Catherine E Bird, 2005 NE 78th St, Kansas City, MO 64118.

Below: *A difficult find – the pheasant was well concealed under the bank among the roots of a fallen tree.*

Show Gundog Qualifying Certificate

In the UK, to obtain the full title of Champion, a gundog must have won three Challenge Certificates (CCs) at Championship Shows under three different judges, and a field trial award or have obtained a Show Gundog Qualifying Certificate. Show Gundog Qualifying meetings are held by breed societies and dogs eligible to enter must have won a CC or a first prize at a Championship Show. Alternatively, a dog having won at least one CC may be tested at a field trial. The requirements for this Certificate are that the dog is not gun-shy, hunts and retrieves tenderly to hand (steadiness is not essential) and enters water where a test is possible.

Obedience

Goldens have a natural flair for obedience and there are many good training clubs where you will initially undertake a 'domestic' obedience course. This involves teaching your dog to walk to heel on and off a lead, sit and stay, recall etc, usually in a hall with the distraction of other dogs and owners. Then you can progress to the more precise work required for competition.

In the UK, the competitive classes are graded as follows: Pre-Beginners, Beginners; Novice, Class A, B C and Championship C. You must gain a qualification in one class before being allowed to compete in the next class. The Golden Retriever's biddable temperament makes it one of the few breeds able to compete at top level with the Border Collie and German Shepherd Dog. The breed's willingness to please enables it to cope with the precision and repetitiveness of this type of competition. In the UK, dogs must win the Champion C Class three times under three different judges with a set number of minimum points to obtain the title of Obedience Champion.

Information concerning your local gundog and obedience training clubs is available from the Kennel Club, together with their Rules and Regulations for Field Trials and Obedience Tests.

Summary of exercises for American Kennel Club Obedience Trials		
Class	**Exercise**	**Max Points**
Novice	Heel on leash	40
	Stand for examination	30
	Heel free	40
	Recall	30
	Long sit	30
	Long down	30
Open	Heel free	40
	Drop on recall	30
	Retrieve on flat	20
	Retrieve over the high jump	30
	Broad jump	20
	Long sit	30
	Long down	30
Utility	Signal exercise	40
	Scent discrimination article 1	30
	Scent discrimination article 2	30
	Directed retrieve	30
	Directed jumping	40
	Group examination	30

Above: *Down and stay exercise. Dogs must remain down for a set time without any extra commands from the handler.*

Below: *Scent discrimination. The dog happily returns to the handler after having found the correct scented cloth.*

In the USA, Obedience Trials are divided into three levels, each level competing for an American Kennel Club obedience title, as follows: Novice – Companion Dog (CD); Open – Companion Dog Excellent (CDX); Utility – Utility Dog (UD).

To gain an AKC obedience title, a dog must earn three 'legs'; each 'leg' requires a score of 170 points out of 200 and more than fifty per cent of points on each exercise. Dogs must have received a Utility Dog title in order to earn points towards an Obedience Trial Championship. Dogs earning a first or second place in Open B or Utility Class (or Utility B, if divided) gain Championship points according to the AKC's schedule of points. An Obedience Trial Champion requires 100 points including a first place in Utility (or Utility B, if divided) with at least three dogs in competition, a first place in Open B with at least six dogs in competition and a third

—— Summary of UK Kennel Club Tests for Obedience Classes ——

Class	Exercise	Max Points
Pre-Beginners	Heel on lead	15
	Heel free	20
	Recall	10
	Sit one minute, handler in sight	10
	Down two minutes, handler in sight	20
Class Beginners	Heel on lead	15
	Heel free	20
	Recall from sit or down	10
	Retrieve an article	25
	Sit one minute, handler in sight	10
	Down two minutes, handler in sight	20
Novice	Temperament test	10
	Heel on lead	10
	Heel free	20
	Recall from sit or down	10
	Retrieve a dumb-bell	20
	Sit one minute, handler in sight	10
	Down two minutes, handler in sight	20
Class A	Heel on lead	15
	Temperament test	10
	Heel free	20
	Recall from sit or down	15
	Retrieve a dumb-bell	20
	Sit one minute, handler out of sight	10
	Down five minutes, handler out of sight	30
	Scent discrimination	30
Class B	Heel free	30
	Send away, drop and recall	40
	Retrieve an article provided by judge	30
	Stand one minute, handler 10 paces or more away	10
	Sit two minutes, handler outof sight	20
	Down 10 minutes, handler out of sight	40
	Scent discrimination	30
Class C	Heel work	60
	Send away, drop and recall	40
	Retrieve an article provided by judge	30
	Distant control – sit, stand and down	50
	Sit two minutes, handler out of sight	20
	Down 10 minutes, handler out of sight	50
	Scent discrimination	50

first, place in either of these.

Goldens in public service

The Golden Retriever also plays many important roles in society as a working and companion dog. He takes a valuable part in search and rescue teams, following disasters such as earthquakes and avalanche where the dog is able to locate survivors in areas either too hazardous or inaccessible to rescuers. Goldens are also used as sniffer dogs, assisting police forces and armies in locating drugs and explosives. As a guide dog for the blind (seeing eye dog), the Golden Retriever has proved invaluable for many years, not only providing seeing eyes for his owner but companionship as well. Goldens also help people with hearing impairments. These 'hearing dogs' keep their charges informed of crucial sounds, eg the telephone, door bell, smoke alarm or a baby's cry. These dogs are literally an extra set of ears. There are many Goldens working as registered PAT dogs as part of an organization which encourages the therapeutic value of dogs to hospitalized and home-bound people.

The Golden Retriever's size, friendliness, great willingness to please and natural retrieving ability means that it is ideally suited to a much newer role as a service and companion dog for the disabled. They carry out many important tasks – carrying small packages on their backs, turning light switches on and off, pushing elevator buttons and pulling wheelchairs.

Below: *The companion/service dog offers more independence to disabled owners, responding to many different commands.*

Appendix

THE BREED STANDARDS
UK
General appearance Symmetrical, balanced, active, powerful, level mover; sound with kindly expression.

Characteristics Biddable, intelligent and possessing natural working ability.

Temperament Kindly, friendly and confident.

Head and skull Balanced and well-chiselled, skull broad without coarseness; well set on neck, muzzle powerful, wide and deep. Length of foreface approximately equal length from well-defined stop to occiput. Nose preferably black.

Eyes Dark brown, set well apart, dark rims.

Mouth Jaws strong, with a perfect, regular and complete scissor bite, ie upper teeth closely overlapping lower teeth and set to the jaws.

Neck Good length, clean and muscular.

Forequarters Forelegs straight with good bone, shoulders well laid back, long in blade with upper arm of equal length placing legs well under body. Elbows close fitting.

Body Balanced, short coupled, deep through heart. Ribs deep and well sprung. Level topline.

Hindquarters Loin and legs strong and muscular, good second thighs, well bent stifles. Hocks well let down, straight when viewed from rear, neither turning in nor out. Cowhocks highly undesirable.

Feet Round and cat-like.

Tail Set on carried level with back, reaching the hocks, without curl at tip.

Gait/movement Powerful with good drive. Straight and true in front and rear. Stride long and free with no sign of hackney action in front.

Coat Flat or wavy with good feathering, dense water-resisting undercoat.

Colour Any shade of gold or cream, neither red nor mahogany. A few white hairs on chest only, permissible.

Size Height at withers: Dogs 56-61cm (22-24in); Bitches 51-56cm (20-22in).

Faults Any departure from the foregoing points should be considered a fault and the seriousness with which the fault should be regarded should be in exact proportion to its degree.

Note: Male animals should have two apparently normal testicles fully descended into the scrotum.

USA
A few years ago, the English Kennel Club insisted that all breed standards should follow the same format, with the same headings and brief descriptions.

The American standard has more lengthy descriptions but basically follows the requirements of the English standard. These are the points which deviate from the English standard.

Head Removal of whiskers permitted but not preferred. (This practice does not occur at all in England.)

Mouth Full dentition required – gaps are considered serious faults. (A scissor bite is the requirement specified in the English Standard.)

Neck Untrimmed natural ruff. (Goldens in England are quite heavily trimmed.)

Body Strong, level topline to sloping croup. (In England a sloping croup would be a fault.)

Colour Not such a broad colour variance allowed in the States compared with the English standard.

Size Different specifications in the States, ie dogs: 23-24 in (58-61cm); bitches: 21-22in (54-56cm).

Weight Dogs: 65-75lb (29.5-34kg); bitches 55-65lb (25-29.5kg).

FURTHER READING
Golden Retriever Today, Valerie Foss, Ringpress.

Third Golden Retriever Book of Champions, Val Foss, Private.

Golden Retriever, Happy Healthy Pet, Cairns, Howell.

The New Golden Retriever, M Schler, Howell.

Golden Retriever, Pet Owner's Guide to, Bargh, Ringpress.

The Golden Retriever, Pepper, TFH.

Golden Retriever, World of the, Nicholas, TFH.

Golden Retrievers, Sucher, Barron.

Golden Retrievers, An Owner's Companion, Anderson, Crowood.

Golden Retrievers, Complete Guide to, Twist, Boydell.

Guide to Owning a Golden Retriever, Huxley, TFH.

A New Owner's Guide to Golden Retrievers, J Laureanoc, TFH.

Golden Retriever, Schneider, Denlinger/BW.

KENNEL CLUBS
Australia Australian National Kennel Council, PO Box 285, Red Hill South, Victoria 3937

Belgium Societe Royale Saint-Hubert, Av. A. Giraud 98-103, Brussels

Canada The Canadian Kennel Club, 89 Skyway Avenue, Etobicoke, Ontario, Canada M9W 6R4

Denmark Dansk Kennelklub, Parkvej 1, Jersie Strand, DK-2680, Solrod, Strand

Finland Suomen Kennelliitto–Finska Kennelklubben, Kamreerintie 8, SF 02770, ESPO

France Societe Centrale Canine, 155 Avenue Jean Jaures, F93535 Paris-

Aubervilliers, Cedex

Germany Verbrand fur das Deutsche Hundewesen (VDH) Westfalendamm 174, Postfach 10 41 54/D44041 Dortmund

Guernsey Guernsey Dog Club, Le Croisy, Icart Road, St Martins, Guernsey C.I.

Holland Raad van Beheer op Kynologisch Gebied in Nederland, Emmalaan 16, PO Box 75091 NL 1070 Ax, Amsterdam,Z

Ireland The Irish Kennel Club Ltd, Fottrell House, Unit 36, Greenmount Office Park, Dublin 6, W

Italy Ente Nazionale Della Cinofilia Italiana, Viale Corsica 20, 1-20137 Milan

Jersey Jersey Dog Club, 1 St Mannelier Close Clairval, St Saviour, Jersey, C.I.

New Zealand New Zealand Kennel Club, Prosser Street, Eldson, Private Bag 50903, Porirua, Wellington

Norway Norsk Kennelklub, Neils Hansens Vei 20, Box 163 Bryn, N 0611, Oslo

Spain Real Sociedad Central de Fomento de las Razas Caninas en Espana, Los Madrazo 20-26, E-28014 Madrid

Sweden Svenska Kennelklubben, S-163 85 Spanga

United Kingdom The Kennel Club, 1–5 Clarges Street, London W1Y 8AB

United States of America American Kennel Club, 51 Madison Avenue, New York, NY 10010

GOLDEN RETRIEVER CLUBS
UK

Golden Retriever Club
Hon Secretary: Mrs J Sparrow,
172 St Neots Road, Sandy, Beds SG19 1BU.
Tel: 01767 682693

All-Ireland Golden Retriever Club
Hon Secretary: Mrs M Gaffney, Tyrol, Kenley Drive, Model Farm Road, Cork, S Ireland.
Tel: 021 345444

Berkshire Downs & Chilterns Golden Retriever Club
Hon Secretary: Mr P Cullen, Aynho Park Lodge, Aynho, Banbury, Oxon OX17 3AX.
Tel: 01869 810605

Eastern Counties Golden Retriever Club
Hon Secretary: Mrs B Webb, Woodbarn, 116 Cambridge Road, Great Shelford, Cambs CB2 5JJ.
Tel: 01223 842358

Midland Golden Retriever Club
Hon Secretary: Mrs F S Stewart, Leigh Court, Leigh, Worcs WR6 5LB.
Tel: 01886 832275

Northern Golden Retriever Club
Hon Secretary: Mrs U Spratt, Cliff Cottage, Lincoln Road, Boothby Graffoe, Lincs LN5 0LB.
Tel: 01522 810797

Golden Retriever Club of Northumbria
Hon Secretary: Mrs A Byrne, 16 Parklands, Hamsterley Mill, Rowlands Gill, Tyne & Wear NE39 1HH.
Tel: 01207 544367

North West Golden Retriever Club
Hon Secretary: Mrs J Robinson, Jojander, 32 Meadowcroft, Euxton, Chorley, Lancs PR7 6BU.
Tel: 01257 264416

Golden Retriever Club of Scotland
Hon Secretary: Mrs M Murray, Treetops Cottage, Kirk Lane, Blair Drummond, Stirling FK9 4AN.
Tel: 01786 841222

Southern Golden Retriever Society
Hon Secretary: Mrs A Stephenson, Timberdown, 33 Guildford Road, Lightwater, Surrey GU18 5RZ.
Tel: 01276 471064

South Western Golden Retriever Club
Hon Secretary: Miss F Coward, Green Acres, Ibsley Drove, Ibsley, Ringwood, Hants BH24 3NP.
Tel: 01425 653146

Ulster Golden Retriever Club
Hon Secretary: Miss E Fearon, 2 Cloverhill Glen, Bangor, Co Down, N Ireland BT16 6XX.
Tel: 01247 45513

Golden Retriever Club of Wales
Hon Secretary: Mr D Roberts, 98 Brynau Wood, Cimla, Neath, W Glams SA11 3YQ.
Tel: 01639 643961

Yorkshire Golden Retriever Club
Hon Secretary: Mrs J Grimmett, 9 Weston Ridge, Otley, W Yorkshire LS21 2EF.
Tel: 01943 465490

USA

Golden Retriever Club of Greater Los Angeles Inc
Jane Jensen, 3250 Rancho El Encino Dr, Covina, CA 91724

Atlanta Golden Retriever Club
Marie Seigler, 208 Milam Rd, Fairburn, GA 30213

White River Golden Retriever Club
Alice Trip, 19490 Lamong Road, Sheridan IN 46069

Garden State Golden Retriever Club
Pat Galante, 23 Cliffview Dr, Augusta, NJ07822

Long Island Golden Retriever Club Inc.
Robert W Young, 548 Ox Path, Bethpage, NY 11714

Dallas-Fort Worth Metro Golden Retriever Club
Kate Thompson, 2703 Coventry Ln, Carrollton, TX 75007

Inland Empire Golden Retriever Club
Marvoureen Daspit, N 505 Farr Rd, Spokane, WA 99206